LIBERTY IN AMERICA, PAST, PRESENT AND FUTURE

A prescription for America.

Dr. Bill Choby

authorHOUSE®

AuthorHouse™
1663 Liberty Drive
Bloomington, IN 47403
www.authorhouse.com
Phone: 833-262-8899

Published by AuthorHouse 10/08/2020

ISBN: 978-1-4520-0083-1 (sc)
ISBN: 978-1-4520-0084-8 (hc)
ISBN: 978-1-4520-0082-4 (e)

Library of Congress Control Number: 2010903450

Print information available on the last page.

Any people depicted in stock imagery provided by Getty Images are models, and such images are being used for illustrative purposes only. Certain stock imagery © Getty Images.

This book is printed on acid-free paper.

Preface:

For nearly 40 years, I have been involved with studying, analyzing and writing about government policies and their effects on American life. I have authored dozens of policy papers and have had over 250 letters to the editor published in a number of local newspapers. I have participated in countless political conversations on talk radio and television forums. I have also spoken at historical and political events including the Tea Party rallies. Yet I only belatedly discovered a passion for politics after establishing a completely unrelated professional career.

My college and professional education was in dentistry. In addition to my Dental Medicine Doctorate, I have another two years of hospital residency and over 1600 hours of continuing education in my field. In 2014 I became board certified in dental implant surgery. In fact, I have more letters after my name than in my name including my middle one! Although I have an substantial amount of training in my chosen field of dentistry, what I can do with my extensive education is subject to government regulation and the unelected bureaucrats who enforce them.

Thanks to the liberal Great Society programs of the 1960s and specifically the Health Manpower Act of 1968, the health care market was swamped by a dramatic increase in new dental graduates, translating into fierce competition within my profession. Never before or since has the federal government pushed for such an increase in the supply of private individual professionals into a stable market of providers.

The Clean Air act of 1970 and the newly created Environmental Protection Agency decimated manufacturing in Western Pennsylvania during the 1970s with intrusive and excessive regulations. The combined effect of these two pieces of federal legislation all of which had a profound impact of my professional career. Needless to say, I have seen the effects of heavy handed government policies from ground zero.

After enduring a bizarre reprimand from the Pa. State Board of Dentistry in 1984 over the placement of a tiny, factually accurate advertisement in the local telephone directory, I felt the full weight of oppressive government action on my career. In a hearing before the Board, the members totally ignored the most fundamental principal of blind justice thereby violating my right to an impartial trial. These politically appointed board members acted as the prosecutor, judge and jury in my deliberations, a galling violation of my constitutionally guaranteed right to due process. To add insult to injury, my attorney failed to file my appeal of the reprimand to a real court of law. My appeal would have easily reversed the board's bogus reprimand, but my attorney's negligence cost me that opportunity. Years later the Pennsylvania Supreme Court overruled a Medical Board decision on the same grounds of denied due process via their commingling of powers in Lyness v Pa. State Board of Medicine. I was right after all, but the bogus reprimand remains a permanent blemish on my record that has haunted my career and cost over one hundred thousand dollars in lost opportunities

Thanks to the Johnstown flood of 1977, excessive environmental regulations, stubborn union bosses, manufacturing losses by Big Steel and restrictions on King Coal, thousands of middle class blue collar workers lost their jobs. Unemployment in my hometown rose to 26% while the political economy was fraught with judicial corruption. The combined effects of a number of legal malfeasants finally forced me to close my practice and file for bankruptcy.

I took nine months off to rethink my career and soon after, I headed back to school to sort out all of the confusion. In less than two years, I earned the very first Masters of Public Administration from Virginia Tech in 1988. While there I studied the nuts and bolts of public policies and their administration at the local, state and national levels. I also extensively studied the due process clause of the 14th amendment in the Federal Constitution and read a number of related Supreme Court decisions. I began to understand just how deep the political disconnection had become back home from the original intent of our rights as Americans.

In 1989, I entered the political scene as an health care policy expert for the City of Johnstown, PA. in a debate over the fluoridation of the town's water supplies. What I discovered was a blatant misunderstanding if not outright contempt for the right of Americans to assemble and voice their dissent. The proposed public health policy would have a direct impact on all of the people, but opponents were restricted in the debate before the members of an unelected municipal authority while elected public officials looked the other way.

Using both my dental background and my masters skills, I concluded that the proposal was foolish and costly. The authority planned on spending over $325,000 to purchase equipment plus tens of thousands more to annually dump 30,000 lbs of fluoride into the local waterways. That's a lot of a potentially toxic chemical to achieve the expected effect of fewer dental cavities in inner city children. My analysis concluded that at a rate on 16 ounces of water per day per child under the age of 12, the collective maximum of the fluoride that could enter the developing teeth of the inner city children was only 5 pounds.

The problem was that poor kids drink more bottled soft drinks than tap water. As a practicing dentist, I see the consequences of the regular consumption of carbonated, sugar laded, acidic sodas on teeth. Its not pretty.

The proponents of this policy planned on paying for this public health intervention with higher monthly water bills. I argued it would be Federally unconstitutional to medicate all people against their will through their water supplies. However, previous court decisions ignored this fundamental right in the name of the public interest. Nonetheless, unelected municipal authority members used the courts to mandate their plan onto the elected but impotent city council. During the course of this public debate, I became an outcast among my colleagues in organized dentistry who supported water fluoridation.

With this experience behind, I decided to become a candidate for U.S. Congress in 1990. I won a contested Republican nomination race, but lost the general election to an incumbent Democrat, John Murtha. However, I came close enough to make him very uncomfortable. I sought a ballot post in 1992, but an partisan judge refused to acknowledge the effects of two snow and ice storms which shut down travel thereby hindering my efforts to secure sufficient nomination signatures on time. I ran again in 1994 and 1996 winning both primary races, but not the general election. I ran unopposed in the GOP primaries 2000 and 2002 only to lose to the same entrenched Democrat. So I moved on and opened a totally new dental practice 25 miles away in Latrobe which I continue to operate today.

During the past 40 years, I have developed a deep sense of appreciation for our nation's founding. I read about the lives of the founding Fathers, visiting numerous historical sites and reviewed countless founding documents. Our forefathers wrote, spoke, and fought against oppressive government for the individual rights to personal freedom in the various colonies. These learned and gifted men were well versed in the theoretical, historical and practical models for personal liberty under government. Their unselfish, God fearing personalities gave them the courage to fight to win their freedom from political bondage. Each were willing and many did sacrifice his own life, liberty and property for the future of a promising land of liberty. These courageous political innovators knew that liberty could only be preserved in our government when the powers of government were contained by the consent of the governed.

Unfortunately, Americans today seem to feel that personal liberty means to do as one pleases. This "do as thou wilst" philosophy is commonly referred to as liberalism. Yet, liberalism is not true liberty. I suspect that most Americans do not really understand the difference between liberalism and liberty. Few Americans today seem to appreciate that it was faith, courage, discipline and personal sacrifice that has made our form of government unique in all of history. It is tragic that many Americans fail to understand that uncontrolled government is the greatest threat to American liberty. Thomas Jefferson once said that "When governments fear the people, there is liberty. When the people fear the government, there is tyranny."

In light of today's enormous expansion of government and its progressively Marxist social agenda, it is my sincere wish that the reader will begin to appreciate the true meaning of liberty. Perhaps the reader will realize as I have, that the foundation of political liberty is rooted in the goodness of its citizens. America's goodness truly comes from its Godliness. I am convinced that the meaning of the Biblical passage which states; "... where the Spirit of the Lord is, there is Liberty." (2 Cor, 3:17) can be understood as personal freedom in America. Hopefully, we the people, will respond to our present crisis in time to secure the blessings of liberty for yet another generation.

This book was written to enlighten the average American as to how we got to where we are today. It also provides a blue print for corrective actions.

Oh yes, and I thanks to my former enemies for birthing a new dimension to my life "for such a time as this".

Willeam Anthony (Bill) Choby BS, DMD, MAGD, MPA, FICCMO DICOI

WHEN MIGHT IS RIGHT, THE PEOPLE GROAN IN BONDAGE.

WHEN RIGHT IS MIGHT, THE PEOPLE ARE FREE.

WHEN RIGHT BECOMES WRONG, THE PEOPLE SUFFER IN CHAOS.

UNTIL RIGHT BECOMES MIGHT AND THE PEOPLE ARE FREE AGAIN.

Contents

CHAPTER 1. LIBERTY, WHAT IS IT?

My country tis of Thee, sweet land of liberty, of Thee, I sing....

The preservation of a free America may well depend upon our ability to check the pulse of liberty's health today. Most of us would be hard pressed to account for the development of personal liberty within the American experience, yet we all speak, read, and exercise these vital freedoms daily. Let us take a look at the different types of liberty.

Physical Liberty; Freedom from bondage or slavery.

Natural Liberty; The unrestricted power for an individual to think, say or do as they choose.

Moral Liberty: Freedom to choose one's own conduct and to bear the consequences of those actions.

Religious Liberty; To worship one's own God without interference.

Political Liberty; The ability of a governing body to manage its affairs according to rules 'freely' selected.

Civil Liberty; Freedom of thought, word or action limited only by self-determined laws that protect each individual member or otherwise benefit all of the individuals affected.

The very concept of a liberated person or society is as old as mankind itself. The birth of liberty was assured when our ancestors realized that they possessed a "free will" and therefore could "choose" alternatives. The healthy development of liberty continued as people recognized the differences between the raw physical laws of survival and the subtle strengths found only in the discipline of respect for one another. Liberty reached adolescence when unrelated people consciously chose to substitute some of their own selfish interests for the stability of a community bound together by laws. These stalwart individuals knew that in order to preserve their society, that they had to sacrifice a portion of themselves. Liberty fully matured when a society accepts a behavioral framework of moral laws and customs within which one could conduct their affairs without recrimination or restraint.

Precisely how would we account for the development of liberty and individual freedom in America today? A number of us would no doubt cite the Declaration of Independence or quote portions of the United States Constitution, while others would probably earmark the Mayflower Compact to make their case. But it is unlikely that many could state how our liberty in America was started.

Perhaps the Colonists had something special in their minds as well as in their hearts, when they inscribed their convictions onto the Liberty Bell nearly two hundred and fifty years ago.

"To proclaim liberty throughout the land and to all of the inhabitants thereof. Leviticus 25:10

Why would the colonists use a quote from the Judeo-Christian Bible to announce their feelings for their new political liberties? Because of all things, the concept of liberty is derived from a long religious tradition of people believing in something greater than themselves, i.e. a higher power or a god.

Can liberty be lost? Yes, indeed!

Liberty is stricken whenever a free people fail to defend it's value. It dies when free people accept the chains of bondage. When brute force or "might becomes right" the ruling powers determine what is right or wrong.

Today all Americans are faced with an unavoidable question:

Are we truly willing to preserve our traditional American forms of individual liberty? Will we stand firm in the conviction that no person or ideology shall be allowed to replace the values and ideals handed down to us by our Founding Fathers? Do we still possess the Spirit of 1776? Are we willing to pay the price of eternal vigilance?

Or will we fritter away our liberties to those who promises to make us equal by dividing us by race, gender, religion and wealth?

So what makes us equal when "We hold these truths to be self evident, that all men are created equal" ???

It is not wealth, gender, race, or religion. It is because we are equally flawed before the perfect God who created us. It is He who makes the truths to be self-evident.

CHAPTER 2. ANCIENT THOUGHTS ON LIBERTY.

Now that we have some idea about the different kinds of liberty, allow me to proceed with a brief review of the history of political theories. This material can be a bit of a challenge to read let alone understand, but bear with me as they are important to gain a full appreciation of what we share in America today.

It is important to understand the how scholars have calculated the centuries before the common era. Researchers were at odds to the exact dates of the early reigns of known kings and pharaohs. It wasn't until Neil Armstrong placed a reflecting mirror on the surface of the moon in 1969 that exact calculations of ancient dates could be made. Scientists can shoot a laser from earth to that mirror and accurately determine the predictably consistent phases of the moon to recreate the celestial sky going back through the centuries of time. By comparing this data with ancient documents that recorded solar or lunar eclipses, an exact calculation of the dates of these events can be made according to our known calenders. The years stated below reflect the corrected calculations so they may appear to differ from other sources.

The earliest records of an alphabet are attributed to the Hebrews in Egypt during the reign of Joseph in 1670 B,C. Recall that his "coat of many colors" that his father, Jacob, had given him caused such jealousy among his 11 brothers that they tried to kill him, but instead sold him into slavery. According to the familiar story, he rose from false imprisonment to prime minister of Egypt because of his ability to interpret the dreams of the Pharaoh. As prime minister, Joseph saved the country from a devastating famine. He became one of the most powerful men in Egypt at that time. Under his administration the Hebrew people grew in numbers and literacy with a new 24 character alphabet to form words that could be written, read or spoken that can be easily understood by others. Instead of symbols, letters and words improved record keeping that could be authenticated centuries later.

The Code of Hammurabi is generally recognized as the oldest set of laws for a city state which was Babylon. Other codes or laws were older but they were mostly among tribesmen. Hammurabi was the King of Babylon from 1560 to 1512 BC. He believed that he was a chosen vassal of the god to establish righteousness in his kingdom. The code addressed very specific applications of law which basically amounted to an eye for an eye and a tooth for a tooth .

When might is right the people groan in bondage.

Written on cuneiform tablets in symbolic characters, the preface of the Code of Hammurabi is as follows;

> *When Anu the Sublime, King of the Anunaki, and Bel, the lord of Heaven and earth, who decreed the fate of the land, assigned to Marduk, the over-ruling son of Ea, God of righteousness, dominion over earthly man, and made him great among the Igigi, they called Babylon by his illustrious name, made it great on earth, and founded an everlasting kingdom in it, whose foundations are laid so solidly as those of heaven and earth; then Anu and Bel called by name me, Hammurabi, the exalted prince, who feared God, to bring about the rule of righteousness in the land, to destroy the wicked and the evil-doers; so that the strong should not harm the weak; so that I should rule over the black-headed people like Shamash, and enlighten the land, to further the well-being of mankind.*

Some scholars argue that the Law of Moses preceded the Code of Hammurabi since there are a number of similarities in the code to the Proverbs of King Solomon. It is mentioned here because self evident truths were universally recognized by virtually all rulers.

The oldest written set of laws destined for western civilization was for a community of liberated people were recorded in 1440 B.C. when the Hebrews were expelled from Egyptian bondage by the Pharaoh. After the Red Sea crossing they followed Moses into the wilderness to Mt Sinai were they were transformed into a nation of people organized under the Ten Commandments as the children of Israel now called Israelis. In the familiar story of Moses on Mount Sinai these laws were carved onto stone tablets by the finger of Yahweh. Nevertheless, the law of God was not easily accepted by them. They quickly returned to their old way so Yahweh left them to wander in the desert until their generation died. 40 years later the next generation of Israelis accepted the Ten Commandments as the legal foundation of their new nationality. The stone tablets were carried in the Ark of the Covenant which symbolized their relationship with God lead the way to many military victories into the promised land of milk and honey. [1]

In addition to receiving the Ten Commandments, Moses wrote other books using the 24 character alphabet of Joseph into a book called the Pentateuch containing rules about virtually every aspect of the lives of the Jewish people. The words written in an alphabetic characters was easy to read by the now literate multitudes to teach the laws of Moses, a significant achievement unto itself. These five books of Moses were added to other historical and prophetic writings of the Jewish culture and combined into one book, the Torah. Over the next several centuries additional material was added to the Torah to form the basis of the Old Testament Bible. It would take several centuries after the death of Jesus Christ before the New Testament Bible was compiled into one book. Some historians believe that the Aramaic version, now called the Peshitta, is the most accurate text of this period. Others point to the Hebrew version. Nevertheless, the Hebrew and Greek translations of these texts eventually became the basis for the Latin, then German and finally the English translations as we know them today.

It may appear that these primitive laws and customs were intended to protect the community from the grim realities of disease, harshness of the environment, or justice between friends and foes. Yet these rules were also designed to liberate those people from their own self-destructive impulses and habits. Under this system of order the supreme authority was the God of Abraham, the ancestral father of the Israelis. The administration of the laws of God were delivered initially by Moses as the Chief Justice. He eventually designed a system of courts with evidentiary standards and judges. He also designated political subdivisions of power from the nation down to the local families. Thus, the concept of a distinct community bound together through written laws and customs and administrated from the bottom up, was born.

Eventually, the law of Moses would become the moral foundation for the three major religions of the world; Judaism, Christianity, and Islam. The overall impact of the adaptation of this world view would affect all civilizations in the world for the rest of our history.

When right is might the people are free.

The next visible attempt at community law can be found in ancient Greece. Most historians agree that the uniquely Western version of community was already in place in Greece during the 5th Century B.C. Prior to this period, most non-religious communities were developed around tribal heads or ethnic kings, i.e. *might is right*, but it was in ancient Greece that the first working model of a democratic government was erected to "create" a society in the interests of the majority of its people.

The most famous of the early Greek philosophers outlining the legal structure of the community/state was a teacher by the name of Plato. His writings are considered to be the first non-religious authority on government and society in the Western world.

Plato's book, The Republic, is a collection of dialogues between Socrates and others who debated the issues of the city/state governance of ancient Greece. Written in 360 BC, Plato attempted to confront the chaos of moral degradation, political confusion and military setbacks that were destroying the ancient Athenian nation. *When right becomes wrong the people suffer in chaos.* In this book Socrates described what he considered to be an "ideal" for the political community. He suggested that political power must reign supreme in order to maintain social order. Plato's theory on the sovereignty of government can be identified in all of the western governments, even to this very day. [2]

In The Republic, the reformer stressed the establishment of political authority as the chief protector of the community; a source of power to be used to protect people from a sometimes hostile world. This ideal government would be based upon the unchanging moral foundations of truth, justice and goodness, that could only be achieved by the application of carefully-structured reason as opposed to the heavy hand of brute force.

This social architect was convinced that this kind of community could liberate the individual to follow his/her needs and aspirations in a social setting where people could live in harmony with nature and others residing there. From Plato's writings emerged the idea of an individual's liberty within the modern political state.

When right is might, the people are free.

Plato considered the basis of social harmony and national strength required a personal conscience and laws that reflected just social values. His book emphasized the individual's personal responsibility for self-control in order to permit personal liberty and social harmony. He wrote;

But in reality justice was such as we were describing, being concerned however, not with the outer man, but with the inward, which is the true self and concernment of man: for the just man does not permit the several elements within him to interfere with one another, or any of them to do the work of the others.---he sets in order his own inner life, and his own law, and at peace with himself... when he has bound all of these together, and is no longer many, but has become one entirely temperate and perfectly adjusted nature, then he proceeds to act, if he has to act, whether in the matter of property, or in the treatment of the body, or in some affair of politics or private business...

Social harmony is the sum and substance of Plato's Republic, providing unity through the spirit of moral justice. The only other conceivable alternative, according to the philosopher, would be attainable through force which is contrary to the concept of liberty.

To operate in tandem with a personal conscience, Plato advised that a community/state should have its one supreme source of authority placed in his conception of the government. The rulers of his society would be segregated into a minority "guardian" class of citizens, who would receive an elite education in the affairs of a proper government.

Plato's system of government demanded an absolute communism, where the needs of the community must take precedence over the rights of the individuals, a perception emphasizing the priority of community property, money and even child rearing in order to perpetuate the social structure he outlined. The enforcement of the elitists' restrictions put upon the common people were considered by the philosopher to be justified to achieve social harmony, with or without personal liberty!

His support for communism was an outgrowth of the argument that only in a community that guaranteed physical protection to its members from its enemies could allow individual liberty to exist.

When might becomes right, the people groan in bondage.

It was in the convulsions of a crumbling Athenian world, where a decline of moral standard and political confusion reigned supreme that Plato created his dream world solution. Perhaps he was, in reality, hoping he would be able to escape the turmoil of his day by imagining a new world order, yet Plato's student, Aristotle, imagined a community that was founded in the reality of daily life where a scientific outlook would prevail for the common man and woman. Aristotle recorded his thoughts in a book, Politics in 350 BC. [3]

In Politics, Aristotle described a political community that took on a more down-to-earth appearance. The philosopher attempted to describe the kind of community that most people would naturally want under the most likely of circumstances. It would be here that people would find the opportunities to realize the liberty to fulfill their personal life goals within a world of political powers.

According to Aristotle, this form of government would provide the means to protect the different customs and traditions unique to its citizens, instead of standardizing them to a form that everyone would be forced to follow. According to this viewpoint, the preservation of the differences between people loomed as an avenue to protect the individual and his family from the total control of the government. In this sense, Aristotle's viewpoints were very similar to those of our own Thomas Jefferson..

Aristotle further argued that the loss of family kinship under Plato's communistic setup would hinder the most useful form of social constraint. Aristotle suggested that love within a closely-knit family would contain anti-social behavior. A society that lacks the respect of close personal relationships would ultimately require the use of force. Sound familiar?

When right is might, the people are free

While Plato called for an absolute communism of property, wealth and families, Aristotle believed that the collective ownership of property, i.e. communism, would encourage people toward irresponsible behavior, since property that is the responsibility of everyone becomes the responsibility of no one. So instead of advocating the development of an ideal state, Aristotle focused on the ideal relationship between social order and good government.

What was important was not the legal structure of government but citizens free to conduct their lives without domination by any form of government. The only road to checking and balancing political power, he urged, was through the influence of religion, cultures and family communities.

In short, the philosopher suggested that preservation of the individual's liberty was a necessary social alternative to repressive collectivism. In other words might is right with big government!

Aristotle's concept of a social order outlined in his book, Politics may also be seen in the political structures of the Western forms of government.

The next evolutionary step in liberty came under the Roman period. The Twelve Tablets of stone, which established Roman law were written in 450 BC following a familiar pattern by declaring standards of right and wrong behavior. Nonetheless, the emperor always had the final word on any matter brought before him. Later Roman Law addressed many other issues of contracts and crime. Yet Roman public law was largely unwritten, instead customs of the ancestors set the parliamentary rules of order that became a model for the rest of western civilization. Roman influences on the structures of our Republic were not accidental. From a standpoint of individual liberty, Romans were barbaric depending on the enslavement of enemies and commoners to sustain the empire. While it appeared that Pax Romani or the peace of Rome was an indication of the legitimacy of its political structure, the Roman government eventually collapsed under the weight of debt, political overreach, and moral degradation of the family and the governing elite.

When might is right the people groan in bondage.
When right becomes wrong, the people suffer in chaos.

CHAPTER 3. CHALLENGES
IN THE MIDDLE AGES.

Following the fall of the Roman Empire, much of Europe was a fragmented collection of countries whose lands were constantly in dispute under the political hierarchies of the sovereign royalties of the kings and queens. The political hierarchy was the feudal system where kings and queens gave portions of their land to bishops and barons in exchange for a regular supply of soldiers and food for the kings. These noblemen subdivided their land to lords who in turn leased it to the peasants who worked for them. Peasants were mostly farmers with few property or individual rights. They were required to pay homage to the lord of the manor in exchange for their protection and the opportunity to tend to their own small plot of land. [4]

When might is right, the people groan in bondage.

The medieval global warming period beginning in the year 800 AD and lasting for 400 years made for a productive climate for growing crops and the preservation of life for man and beasts. The principal food staples were essentially beans, barley, nuts, berries, rye and wheat grains that were vulnerable to adverse weather and invading armies. Yet, hunger still was a daily reality for the serf farmers who paid homage with the fruits of their labors to the manor. Malnutrition and infectious communicable diseases reminded them that death was never far away from their doorsteps. Uncertain food supplies were a regular cause of political conflict and wars. Individual freedom was virtually unheard of at the time. It was survival of the fittest in a brutish short life with primitive living conditions and nearly constant wars among the kings ancestry nobility. [5]

The near constant political tumult among the landowners created a niche for other forms of influence. Religious leaders had influence beyond the political borders but within the boundaries of 3 distinct religions. Although the Jews, Christians and Arabs were distant kinsmen by their common ancestry to the Patriarch Abraham, they differed significantly in matters of doctrine. The connection between them was by Ismail, the eldest son of the Patriarch Abraham and Hagar, who was the handmaid of Sarah, Abraham's wife. Abraham's second son, Isaac by Sarah is considered the father of the Jewish nation and eventually all Christians. But that's where the similarity ends. Centuries later, bitter violence in the name the Abraham's God continues today.

When right becomes wrong, the people suffer in chaos.

The Arabs claimed the City of Jerusalem as their spiritual capital as did the Jews and Christians. When the Arabs seized control of the Temple of Solomon in Jerusalem, armies from Christian Europe crusaded to take it back. The Crusades ended with mixed results. Early In the 12th century, nine dedicated elite soldiers organized to liberate the Holy Lands from the Arabs. They called themselves the Poor Knights of the Temple of King Solomon, but they became known as the Knights Templar. When Christians made their pilgrimage to the Holy Land, the knights went along as protectors. The Templars gradually found favor in the eyes of the Roman Catholic Church. So in 1130, Pope Innocent II issued a papal bull recognizing the pious warriors as a monastic order thereby allowing them to operate across all political borders. Following a strict oath of Christian virtues and a military code of conduct to they grew in numbers attracting power and wealth.

> *[A Templar Knight] is truly a fearless knight, and secure on every side, for his soul is protected by the armor of faith, just as his body is protected by the armor of steel.*

> *He is thus doubly-armed, and need fear neither demons nor men.*

The Templars soon possessed great wealth as new recruits voluntarily surrendered their wealth to the Order as an initiation requirement into the membership. Soon their numbers exceeded 10,000 making them the largest military force in Europe. Peasants enjoyed more freedom under the protection of the Templars than the local kings. They extended their activities into agriculture, banking, commerce owning over 9000 tracts of land.

When right is might, the people are free.

Over time, the Templar economy embarrassed the authority of the kings and the Catholic Church. Jealous monarchs put political pressure onto the Catholic church which in turn charged the Templars with heresy, an accusation worthy of death. One of the accusations involved the knights' worship of a cloth of a bearded man, possibly the Shroud of Turin. On Friday the 13th, 1307, the Templar's Grand Master and 60 of this officers were killed or captured and tortured until confessions condemned them to execution. The persecutions continued for 7 years. The remaining Grand Master, Jacques de Molay was burned at the stake March 18th, 1314 after he recanted a previous forced guilty confession. Legend has it that De Molay laid a curse on the French King Philip and Pope Clement prophesying that both men would die within a year. True to the word, both Pope Clement V and Philip IV died within the year. The Templars who escaped fled to Scotland and Portugal. Legend has it that the knights carried and buried the Holy Grail taken from King Solomon's Temple in Rosalyn Chapel in Scotland. Recent reports by the Vatican indicate that the Knights carried the Shroud of Turin to France after the fall of Constantinople. Friday the 13th remains as an omen of bad luck even to this day.

When right becomes wrong, the people suffer in chaos.
Until right becomes might and the people are free again.

The most important first step in the negotiations of personal freedoms in Western cultures that were recognized and defended by a government was the Magna Carta in 1215. The agreement came most reluctantly when King John of England was facing near certain defeat of his army at Runnymead. To avoid a disaster, King John agreed to recognize the unwritten rights of man. Although far from perfect, the charter was a written promise that the king would share some of his sovereign monarchy with his subjects.

Enter the little ice age in 1300 where global cooling caused glaciers to move south into the northern latitudes. For the next 500 years, climate changes had a profound effect of the political economy of northern Europe. Survival required changes in agriculture and forced population to migration in search of food and shelter. As technology developed improved means of transportation, people went into motion to find a more predictable way of life. [6]

In 1330 a bubonic plague spread from China to Europe. In five years 1/3 of the population of Europe, an estimated 25 million people died from the black death, The causalities from the plague caused a shortage of laborers who demanded higher pay but the lords of the manor often refused. Riots and plundering soon followed. Religious leaders were at loss to explain why so many followers' prayers were not answered. The faithful began to rethink their doctrines and beliefs. [7]

Just as mysteriously as the black death appeared, it also disappeared as people move away from the plague ridded cities into the isolated countryside. The decades of disease, weather related famine, and war challenged the political hierarchy as lords and noblemen struggled for life along with the peasants. Anarchy reigned supreme.

When right becomes wrong, the people suffer in chaos.

By 1492, the remnant Templars in Portugal were renamed The Knights of Christ to conceal their past ties with the Templar persecution. They remained organized as a clandestine society and created a secret symbol to identify themselves. That symbol was the letter X with a horizontal dash on the top left of the right diagonal. Legend has it that the father of Christopher Columbus joined the secret order and brought his son Christopher into the order. Christopher married the daughter of one of their Grand Masters. The proof of his membership lay in his writings which included the secret hooked X. Further evidence may be the Templar red 'patte' cross symbol on the sails fo the Nina, Pinto, and the Santa Maria. As a Knight of Christ, Christopher would have likely learned of the seafaring exploration by the Scottish Templar remnant to new lands in the western Atlantic Ocean. The very same day that he set sail, Spain's Queen Isabella ordered all Jews to leave Spain or be killed. Columbus subsequent voyages were funded by money confiscated from the Jews by the queen.

When might is right, the people groan in bondage.

A monumental shift in political thought emerged during that period of history. It came to be called the Reformation because reform was needed after the failures of the church hierarchy to walk the talk on matters of faith. In 1611, England's King James III ordered the translation of the Holy Bible from the ancient languages to common English. The book shook the political world from its moorings in a way that could not have been imagined. Although John Calvin and Martin Luther were responsible for taking the Words of Scripture to the masses, it was the King James Translation that caused a keen interest in the kingdom or the government of God on earth. For now, as never before or since, the common people had individual access to precisely defined political and personal laws of liberty from the Judeo-Christian heritage. Biblical law had an impact upon society that quickly revolutionized the world.

It was during this period of time that people began to question the "Divine right" of Kings to rule over people. This often quoted interpretation taken from the book of Genesis stated that God gave kings dominion over their lands because God gave dominion to Adam in the garden of Eden. These clever monarchs pointed to their blood lines as being directly descendant from Adam as the source of their authority, when in fact that all men are descendants of Adam.

An English scholar recognized the fallacy of the sovereignty claim by the royalty. In 1644, Rev. Samuel Rutherford wrote <u>The Law and the Prince</u>. In his text, Rutherford argued that men's laws should be based upon the Word of God rather than the forever changing words of man. Rutherford held that all men, including kings, were under the law and could not exempt their own actions from the sovereignty of the law. By this line of reasoning the age-old problem of absolute sovereinty was solved. Since Adam and Eve's fall in the garden, every human being fell short under the perfect justice of a sovereign God. Now because every human being was imperfect, people became equal by their common imperfection. In other words, all people were equal before the judgement of God. So in a society of laws that used the perfect justice of God as a standard, people were equal to one another. Citizens would then be entitled to equal rights in relation to the perfect standards of justice. The King James Bible provided the solution to the problem of supreme authority that had perplexed political philosophers for ages. The seed was planted, but it would take decades to plant roots deep into the public conscience. [8]

When right is might the people are free.

Another prominent political writer of the time was Thomas Hobbes the author of the <u>Leviathan.</u> Written in 1651, <u>Leviathan</u>, which literally means a huge beast, we discover that Hobbes' selection of this title was quite appropriate. Considered to be one of history's foremost originators of political theories, Hobbes' concocted notions about political order that were seen as a direct attempt to solve England's problems of social disorder. Conflicts between the citizen and the existing laws was continuous and destructive. His ideas came on the heels of a rigid control of all social groups under the reign of King Henry the VIII.

The most famous of King Henry's power plays was his calculated breaking with the supreme authority of the Roman Catholic Pope. He seized control of the church in England and appointed himself in charge. Embracing a similarly ruthless view toward any differences of opinion in society, Hobbes insisted that government must control everything in order to be effective in maintaining order. In effect, Hobbes emphasized that government must actually be a huge beast in order to work properly. Hobbes believed that man's natural tendency is to do unto others before they do to you. He considered man's life accurately described as "...solitary, poor, nasty, brutish and short."

When might is right, the people groan in bondage.

With this notion in mind, Hobbes believed that the only way a governing body could control these natural tendencies in order to create social order rested in forcibly containing basic instincts. His primary goal in his philosophical writing was to propose the acceptance of absolute power as a cure for civil wars, crimes and other anti-social behavior, where man's destructive primitive instincts are released.

However we need to ask these vital questions: Who is to determine what constitutes the law? By what standard will it be administered? Hobbes answers were that law would be the command of the sovereign king. He also stressed that the law is;

> *...to every subject, those Rules which the Commonwealth hath Commanded him, by Word, Writing, or other sufficient Sign of the Will, to make use of, for the Distinction of Right and Wrong.*

It is clear to us that if the civil laws proposed by Hobbes were to be at the discretion of man. They would conflict painfully with the moral laws of the Judeo-Christian tradition. What is equally clear is that we would expect Hobbes to literally hate religious institutions because of this conflict. Hobbes reasoned;

> *For seeing the Ghostly Power challengeth the Right to declare what is Sinne (sin) it challengeth by consequence to declare what is Law.*

Here, sins against God were viewed as transgression of religious laws which could become the basis of man-made laws. In other social matters, this philosopher considered the family as an extension of this heavy-handed use of authority and recommended replacing the natural authority of the father and mother with the authority of the state.

It may seem odd to us that Thomas Hobbes would believe, in his wildest imaginings, that absolute authority is the only way to secure liberty for the individual. He actually believed that if man's instincts were to be contained by sovereign civil laws, it would then follow that man would be liberated to become his real self.

Hobbes contributed to the development of individual liberty in America by formulating the notion of placing ultimate social power into government's legal framework and thereby sheltering it from the ever changing minds of kings. Hobbes' ideas on supreme law provided the seed for the next evolutionary step in our liberty; law to be created by the General Will of the people. [9]

On of the most influential writings on American liberty, was penned as a discussion on modern civil government by John Locke in 1689. Locke's <u>Second Treatise on Government</u> carefully built his case for political leadership by the consent of the governed by once again meticulously referring to the very same Bible. Locke, an English physician turned philosopher, expounded on the rights of citizens to life, liberty and property as a fundamental gift from God Himself. The moral foundations of civil and criminal laws would arise from the good of the community. [10]

In Chapter II, Of the State of Nature., Locke wrote;

Chapter 2, Sect. 4. TO understand political power right, and derive it from its original, we must consider, what state all men are naturally in, and that is, a state of perfect freedom to order their actions, and dispose of their possessions and persons, as they think fit, within the bounds of the law of nature, without asking leave, or depending upon the will of any other man.

Chapter 2. Sect. 6. But though this be a state of liberty, yet it is not a state of licence: though man in that state have an uncontroulable liberty to dispose of his person or possessions, yet he has not liberty to destroy himself, or so much as any creature in his possession, but where some nobler use than its bare preservation calls for it. The state of nature has a law of nature to govern it, which obliges every one: and reason, which is that law, teaches all mankind, who will but consult it, that being all equal and independent, no one ought to harm another in his life, health, liberty, or possessions: for men being all the workmanship of one omnipotent, and infinitely wise maker; all the servants of one sovereign master, sent into the world by his order, and about his business; they are his property, whose workmanship they are, made to last during his, not one another's pleasure: and being furnished with like faculties, sharing all in one community of nature, there cannot be supposed any such subordination among us, that may authorize us to destroy one another, as if we were made for one another's uses, as the inferior ranks of creatures are for our's. Every one, as he is bound to preserve himself, and not to quit his station wilfully, so by the like reason, when his own preservation comes not in competition, ought he, as much as he can, to preserve the rest of mankind, and may not, unless it be to do justice on an offender, take away, or impair the life, or what tends to the preservation of the life, the liberty, health, limb, or goods of another.

Following the introduction of the concept of sovereign law as the supreme authority in governments, another step in the ongoing development of political philosophy was taken by an 18ᵗʰ Century Frenchman by the name of Rousseau. This man became one of the leading figures during the French Enlightenment.

In 1762, Rousseau wrote <u>Social Contracts</u>, where he put forth the idea of the "General Will" as the ultimate expression of a community's people. This philosophical idea placed the wishes of the majority of a community's people in the role of determining their laws or democratic sovereignty. "Demo" refers to the majority of people while "cratic" refers to a form of government. [11]

Considering sovereignty as meaning absolute authority, Rousseau connected Hobbes' idea of the absolute state with the will of the masses of people in his recipe for providing individual freedoms. Rousseau viewed the general will or what he termed the voice of the people as just and equitable since it could be equated to the wisdom of the masses. This concept was taken to the extreme in the popular slogan "vox populi, vox Dei which meant that the majority opinion of the people was the voice of God. This somewhat foolish distortion of God attracted many followers. However, like so many other failed ideas that begin by mixing truth with lies, Rousseau's community didn't last long.

It was rather high minded idealism that the will of the masses did not mean mob rule. Nevertheless, Rousseau felt that open discussion among all of the people would reveal the "right" answers on questions of law or politics. The argument was flawed in that common knowledge or for that matter, common sense does not always equate with true wisdom.

The problem with this kind of enlightened community according to Rousseau was that people could not be free to discuss their ideas and laws until the rigors of life were removed by a powerful central government.

Remember that France in the 1700's was the focal point of a new philosophy known as the Enlightenment. This new age of reasoning pitted reason against tradition, secularism against religion and singular political power against a host of power sources. Hence it was an age when philosophers like Rousseau greatly detested the political and social power of the Christian church because they were unable to control the followers of Christ with their "new" ideas concerning the general will.

He considered the Christian commitment to their faith as a major obstacle to the people's committing allegiance to the state. He wrote;

> *Each citizen would then be completely independent of all his fellow men, and absolutely dependent on the state; which operation is always brought by the same means; for it is only by the force of the state that the liberty of its members can be secured.*

Unfortunately for us freedom lovers, what Rousseau calls freedom is nothing more than freedom to do what the state determines to be acceptable, at least until such time as the majority changes its mind regarding what is or isn't acceptable.

On matters pertaining to family, Rousseau believed that the parents should not be permitted to educate their children because a father's prejudices would interfere with the development of good citizens. His reasoning for this far-reaching conclusion was;

> *Should the public authority, in assuming the place of the father and charging itself with this important function, acquire his rights in the discharge of his duties, he should have little charge to protest, for he would only be altering his title, and would have in common, under the name citizen, the same authority over his children, that he was exercising separately under the name of father, and would be no less obeyed when speaking in the name of the law then when he spoke in that of nature.*

In Rousseau's viewpoint, society should coerce children to conform to the outlook of the majority of people. This objective could not be achieved when parents had any authority over their children. We may now appreciate why history has revealed governments placing its will in direct opposition to families and religions. These three authorities possess vastly different notions regarding who should have the last say or wield the supreme authority over a society's people.

Rousseau's "general will" did have its opportunity to be tested by the fire of experience. This test came in the form of the French revolution. Contrary to what many may think of this period of governmental theory in action, it really was anarchy, or the complete lack of governmental order. The general will became unabridged freedom to do as one saw fit. When the general will became provoked by shortages of food, a mob stormed the Bastille and ended the absolute monarchy of King Louis XVI.

When right becomes wrong, the people suffer in chaos.

The general will had become a mob mentality. Ironically, King Louis XVI sought to end the cycles of famine that fueled the mob by encouraging the French people to eat potatoes. He had introduced potatoes as an experiment using armed guards to protect the field of growing plants. With the tacit approval of the King, hungry farmers began to steal the plants for their own use. Marie Antoinette wore potato flowers in her hair which soon became a fashion trend among other women of France. However the political benefits of the King's food was undiscovered until after the bloody French revolution had ended the Monarchy. The revolt, not surprisingly, was primarily due to famine brought upon the failed grain crops during the cold storms of the little ice age in Europe. The rest of the European countries who had already accepted the potato had realized that the tubers growing underground were protected from adverse weather and the feet of armies. However in France, the benefit was only realized after much unnecessary blood had been shed. The economic chaos, random violence and eventually a European war became a historical tribute to the failed philosophy of the "Do as thou wilst".

CHAPTER 4. THE NEW WORLD.

During the Medieval Global warming period around 1000 AD, Viking explorers settled the islands west of the British Isles. Since the climate was agreeable to agriculture, Norse settlements were established first on Iceland then onto Greenland, so named "green" because it had a suitable climate. Some evidence suggests that the Vikings landed on the North American continent. As the temperatures began to drop from the global cooling of the little ice age, these early settlements were gradually abandoned driving the settlers back to the European mainland.

The previously discussed fate of the Knights Templar left the Order in tatters. Persecution had scattered the warrior monks with many of them seeking refuge in Scotland and Portugal. In Scotland, the knights joined with the Sinclair family and established themselves as a military force and expeditionary explorers. In search of a new Jerusalem their seafaring journeys carried them to North America 100 years before Columbus.

In 1398, Templar Knight Prince Henry Sinclair landed on Oak Island. Nova Scotia and attempted to establish a foothold in the new land. From this base, he explored the eastern Atlantic coast claiming the land for the Order of the Templars. Stone markers from the explorers have been found in Westford, Connecticut, Spirit Pond, Maine, and The Narragansett Rune Stone off the shores of Rhode Island. A stone tower was constructed near today's Newport,

RI to mark the winter solstice much like Stone Henge in England. The Newport tower is a medieval structure with carefully placed openings which when aligned points west to another discovery of a stone marker, the Kensington Ruse Stone in the land south of the Great Lakes in what is now Minnesota. The Templars explorers etched all of these stone with words that included the secret marker; the hooked X as proof of their land claims in North American. The Templar settlements in America eventually were abandoned as global cooling during the little ice age made the lands inhospitable. [12]

The Scottish Templar knights evolved into the Fraternal Society of Free Masons because of their skills as stone masons. The decedents of this secret society played an important role in establishing a New Jerusalem in America. George Washington was a Free Mason as well as 1/3 of the signers of the Declaration of Independence. The concept of separation of state from church first exercised by the Templars, came from their decedents, the Masons, in what became another revolutionary idea in the evolution of liberty.

When Columbus re-discovered America in 1492 his greater achievement was in finding a new path to reach the new world. In doing so, he debunked the superstitions of ancient mariners who imagined terrifying horrors that lay awaiting in the uncharted waters of the western Atlantic Ocean. Columbus's southern route was more distant but it had more predictable weather patterns than the northern routes of the Templar explorers 100 years earlier. Below the equator, Columbus followed the natural westerly flow of the trade winds. On return voyages, he navigated north of the equator where the eastward winds carried him back to Portugal. Although the latitude was prone to hurricanes, the waters were navigable for most of the year. This discovery opened the floodgates of trade to the wealth of land, new types of food, raw materials, and precious metals. The abundance of new wealth had a profound effect on the political economies of Europe.

The trade winds discovered by Columbus quickly lead to further exploration of the Americas. European ships carried manufactured goods to the settlements in the Americas and returned with new raw materials and foods. Among these early foods were a variety of potatoes from Peru that became a reliable food source in Europe. By the early 1600s, potatoes were growing in most of Europe, although many thought the tubers were poisonous and demonic because they grew below the ground. The slow rate of acceptance was particularly noted in France where many believed that the potatoes were the cause of many deadly diseases such as leprosy and the black plague. The superstition was so wide spread that the food was actually outlawed in much of the country.

With a more dependable food source of the potatoes, populations rebounded from the previous losses of disease and wars all over Europe. The growing populations ushering in an age of Renaissance and exploration. Being somewhat relieved of famine and plagues of disease, people had more time for other pursuits such as religion, science and political discourse. [13]

Doctrinal religious differences between Protestants and Catholics sparked persecution of the conflicting loyalties to the Pope and the Protestant Bible. The Protestant clergy was armed with the recently printed King James Bible, thanks to Gutenberg's invention of the printing press. The Roman Catholic church who claimed direct dependency from St. Peter depended on Canon Laws and the infallibility of Papal edicts as their supreme authority. Since the conflicting issues involved how one's soul would spend eternity, the discussions were predictably intense and political.

The confusing doctrines quickly became apparent to the faithful who began to seek the Truth on their own. As Bibles became more plentiful, differing interpretations of the Word soon followed leading to challenges of religious leaders. Not surprisingly, persecution forced the faithful to seek refuge into isolated communities. The acceptable rules of living under God were gleaned from the Bible including the belief that people were liberated from the ravages of sin though the resurrection of Jesus Christ. These developments in religious freedom gradually lead to a desire to expand their freedom to other activities of life including their form of governance. Common law emerged as a consensus of common sense morality based on the growing influence of religion in the common man.

For the next century, between 1500 and 1600, English and French explorers mapped the North American continent while the Spanish and Portugese explored South America. While the native Americans claimed ownership of the new world as a gift from the Great Spirit, there were no set boundaries. The warriors from the six nations of the Iroquois claimed their land by conquest. The British and the French either seized the land or bought it for a mere pittance of its value from the natives. When French and British kings claimed title by exploration, the land was opened to be surveyed and sold or granted to anyone laying a claim from their respective home countries.

CHAPTER 5. EARLY
AMERICAN HISTORY.

The development of liberty in America has many historical roots, but there were some key incidents without which it is doubtful that it would have ever developed into our constitutional rule of law which guarantees individual liberty to American citizens.

In 1603, King James of England issued a claim on all of the land west of the Middle Atlantic shores into the interior of the undiscovered continent of the new World. Following a grant from the King, Jamestown was established in Virginia in 1604. Although the settlement eventually failed, the English had established a presence on the Continent. Later pilgrims from religious oppression in England secured a grant to also establish a colony in Virginia. Fierce storms pushed their little ship, the Mayflower off course to the north forcing them to land on Cape Cod. Many of the pilgrims travelers were stricken with illness and some died, but enough survived to establish the colony of Plymouth in the early winter of 1627. Searching for a suitable location to live, they found land cleared of trees and brush already prepared for planting. The land had been cleared by the natives, but was abandoned by them because of an epidemic of small pox introduced by contact with English explorers. The native settlement of Patuxet was believed to be cursed of disease, but to the Pilgrims it was a godsend. The small band of immigrants sought to live out their Gospel of pure Christianity without persecution in the new world. These Pilgrims to the new world manage to survive the winter losing half of their members to sickness, hunger and the elements. The future of the colony appeared to be hopeless.

The following spring a English speaking native brave appeared out of the short pine woods. Squanto had been captured as a lad by English slave traders and taken to back to Spain where he was rescued from the slave block by monks. The monastery raised him and educated him in their language. When he boy turned to man he moved to England where he learned the ways of the English along with their language. Eventually he managed to find passage across the ocean back to his American home on the shores of the Atlantic. Squanto befriended the struggling pilgrims and instructed them in planting corn and catching eels in the low tide. In effect, he prevented he starvation of the famished settlers and saved the colony. [14]

English and French sea captains had been exploring the eastern coast and inland waterways of America for over 100 years. In 1642, French explorer LaSalle sailed the Great Lakes in search of moving water ways south into the interior of the continent. After a short portage from the south shore of Lake Errie, he located a deep stream running south which he promptly named French creek The English called the same waterway the Beef River. The stream eventually drained into a larger river, the Allegheny also known as La Belle Rive or the beautiful river to the French. The Allegheny joined the northward flowing Monongahela River to form the Ohio river which connected with the Mississippi that flowed into the Gulf of Mexico. During his exploration La Salle claimed all of the land that drained into these waterways for France. French fur traders and Catholic missionaries began to settle the raw wilderness.

While the French and English explorers laid claims to the lands west of the Allegheny mountains, there was a third nation with even older roots, the Six Nations of the Iroquois. The federation of six native American tribes consisting of Mohawks, Oneidas, Onondagas, Cayugas, Senecas and eventually the Tuscaroras. They were warriors who had a loosely defined nation that ruled their people by what can be described as participatory representative democracy based on a novel concept, government by the consent of the governed.

However if anyone opposed them they put their lives at risk. In the Ohio country, the Delawares, Shawnees, Mingos, Monogehalians and other small tribes were more peaceful and were more concerned with growing crops of corn, beans and squash. [15]

For decades the natives traded peacefully with the Europeans. The natives called the French father in deference to the Catholic missionary priests, while the English were called brothers. However with three governments laying claim to much of the same lands a die was cast for an what would become the eventual military showdown for land rights.

Perhaps the first blow to the fragile peace between the nations was struck in a little known incident that occurred around the year 1720. In an transaction dispute, French fur traders seized a Seneca man and his young son, Tanacharison, in what is now upstate New York. The helpless boy watched in horror as the traders tortured his father to death. They subsequently boiled and ate the remains before the young man whose life was spared. The act of unimaginable brutality to the captive native branded hatred deep into the heart of this terrified youth. A passion for revenge would never be forgotten and determined to arise when the opportunity presented. The lad grew up to become a tribal chief and later was selected by the Council of the Iroquois Confederation to be a half king to engage in diplomacy talks with the English. The title identified him as a sort of governor in the Ohio country. [16]

Around 1750, the French military began to expand their presence in the Ohio country by building a series of fortifications along the waterways previously claimed for France by the explorer LaSalle over 100 years earlier. The first of these forts was established at Presque Isle on the southern shore of Lake Erie. The second of these forts lay at the headwaters of Beef Creek and was appropriately called Fort LeBeuf or Fort Buffalo by the french since these beasts were commonly found in the area. To witness their claims, the french soldiers planted lead plates near the junctions of the tributaries with the rivers. The French supposed that any land that drained its water into these waterways were also part of their land claim. In effect the

French believed that they owned all of the land west of the Allegheny mountain range.

As the French military construction was undertaken on another fort on the Allegheny River, word trickled back through the local natives to the English settlers in the vicinity. The message eventually found its way back to Williamsburg and the English Virginian investors who were planning on developing the Ohio country. Recall that the English claimed these same territory under the King James charter in 1603. The English claim extended to northwest to Lake Erie and beyond to the shores of the Mississippi River. This large area was considered to be the western part of Virginia. The specific area around the three rivers of th Allegheny, the Monongahela and the Ohio were eventually made into Augusta County, Virginia.

The investors in the land speculation included a young George Washington who had surveyed much of the land east of the Allegheny mountains and below the Potomac River as an apprentice for Lord Fairfax. George grew up as a neighbor to the Fairfax family, later to become a close friend with the Lord Fairfax by assisting him surveying his huge land grant in the western parts of Virginia. George also joined Fairfax in pursuit of the oldest organized sport in America, fox hunting with horses and hounds. It was during the frequent outings on horseback, that George became an accomplished rider with a deep love for the sport and the land he hunted. Washington's fox hunting ties introduced him to the land owning and therefore powerful, country gentry. Relations with the fox hunting fraternity would later prove to be a gateway to future political opportunities for the ambitious youth.

When Virginia Governor Dinwiddle, sought an emissary to approach the French in the Ohio country, George Washington was a natural selection. Proven to be able to survive the raw elements of the backwoods, Washington set out as a 21 year old major of the Virginia Regiment with a letter from Dinwiddle to politely inform the French commander at Fort LeBeuf that he was in Western Virginia. Along the way, George enlisted the help of Christopher Gist, a trader/settler familiar with the western lands. Gist was a character not unlike the fictitious character, Hawkeye of James Fenimore Cooper's classic book Last of the Mohicans. Gist and Washington set out from Winchester, Virginia then onto Wills Creek, currently Cumberland, Maryland, where they followed Nemacolin's path, a native American trail from the headwaters of the Potomac to the Monongahela river.

Washington's wrote that "he knew of no person so well qualified for the undertaking as Capt. Gist. He has extensive dealings with the Indians, is in great esteem with them, and well acquainted with their manners and customs. He is indefatigable, patient, most excellent qualities where the Indians are concerned. And for his capacity and zeal I dare venture to engage."

Washington and Gist made way to the forks of the three rivers, the Allegheny, the Monongahela and the Ohio noting its potential strategic military value. At Loggs town a small native town, 20 miles south of the three rivers' fork on the north shore of the Ohio, the travelers met Tanacharison, the appointed diplomat for the Ohio Country. The Half King was a member of the Mingo tribe, with ties to the Six Nations of the Iroquois who had settled into the area. Tanacharison was now an adult warrior whose father was murdered by French traders as previously mentioned.

Washington, Gist, Half King and a few others made their way to the French Fort LeBeuf, where George delivered Gov. Dinwiddle's letter to the French Commandant. After two long days, he received a written reply. The French response was cordial, but a curt refusal to vacate the territory. With his mission completed, Washington and Gist set out for a return trip to Williamsburg. After two days the horses became so weak from hunger that the men left them behind and set out on foot. One of the natives who was guiding Washington and Gist through the wilderness, suddenly turned and fired his musket at Washington from only a few yards away. Fortunately, he missed and was quickly disarmed and eventually released. George and Christopher set out on their own. They walked the rest of that day and into the night until they arrived at the north shore of the Allegheny river near the forks of the Ohio. They spent the better part of a day making a raft with only a small hatchet. By later afternoon they set out into the river while large blocks of ice complicated the crossing. Hoping to avoid being capsized, George stuck his pole into the strong current when it became jammed between rocks. The sudden effect threw young George into 10 feet of freezing river water. Gist managed to get him on board while they struggled to get to an island in the middle of the river. With overnight temperatures in the mid 20s, Gist suffered frostbite on his fingers. Washington survived in spite of being soaking wet the evening before. By morning, the ice had frozen solid enough for them to walk off the rest of the way across the river to solid land. Major George arrived in Williamsburg in January 1754 after traveling over 900 miles in three months. The record of Washington's journal of his 1753 trip can be read in its entirety online in the national archives. [17]

Major George Washington was promoted to Lt. Colonel and sent back the Ohio country in the spring on 1754 to establish a fort at the point of the three rivers. When he arrived he found the French had the same idea and had already built their Fort Duquense. Frustrated George sent a messenger back to Dinwiddle and marched back to the Great Meadows on the Laurel Mountain plateau near the Nemacolin trail.

The following map was printed in the London Magazine in 1754 showing the 900 mile journey path of Major George Washington from Williamsburg to Fort LeBeuf and back. [18]

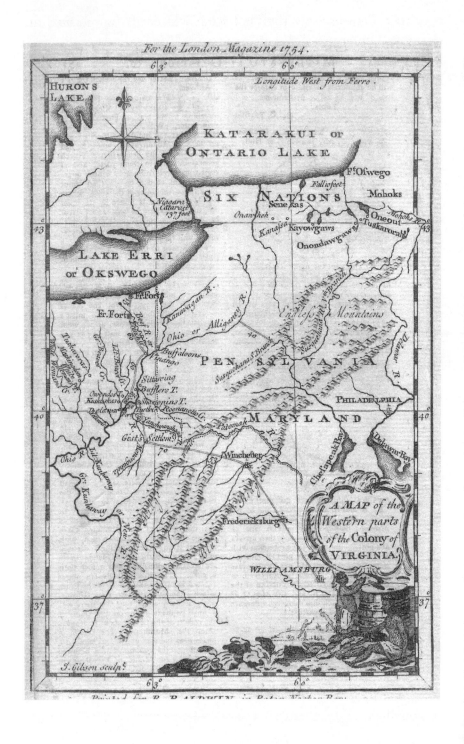

For the London Magazine 1754.

Enter Tanacharison, the Half King with an advanced warning about an approaching French band of soldiers intending to attack Washington. Believing the native warrior, Washington prepared a pre-emptive strike. Following Half King on a narrow trail through the dense forest in a all night rain assured the inexperienced Washington the element of surprise. At dawn, the French soldiers were just waking up when they found themselves completely surrounded by Washington's men and Tanacharison's warriors. One of the French soldiers who had walked away from the encampment to relive himself watch in disbelief. Washington, who was itching for a fight, thanks to the urging of Tanaharison, ordered his company to open fire. 13 Frenchmen were killed and 21 captured with Washington losing only one dead and three wounded. The Frenchman who escaped by nature's call, ran barefoot back to Fort Duquense with news of the attack.

When the hostilities ceased, the wounded leader of the French detachment, Ensign Joseph Coulon de Jumonville was propped up against a tree. He vehemently protested the action as an unprovoked surprise attack. In his pocket was a letter calling for the British to leave the French territory. He claimed that he was simply on a diplomatic mission, not unlike Washington's earlier visit to Fort LeBeuf. Jumonville argued that the lack of French sentry guards over their camp as evidence of his nonviolent mission. Seizing an opportunity, perhaps to exact revenge for the tortuous death of his father by other Frenchmen, Tanacharison sunk his tomahawk into the head of Jumonville while saying; "Vous n'êtes pas mort encore mon père!" translated into "Thou are not dead yet, my father.". The blow kill Jumonville instantly. Half King then removed his victim's brains and washed his hands in them George reacted to the cold blooded murder of this well intended French officer by retching in angst. French blood had been shed in the rugged mountain glen that would set the future of America on a collision course with destiny. [19]

Sensing certain hostilities, Washington returned to Great Meadows to build a defensive Fort out of Necessity and to await supplies and re-enforcement from Wills Creek. The French commander of Fort Duquesne, Captain Louis Coulon de Villiers, Jumonville's half-brother set out to exact a measure of his own revenge.

The French and natives soon had Washington's men surrounded in their hastily erected colonnade of logs and trenches. The small fort lay in a depression in an open field because Washington expected an open confrontation in the classic European manner of warfare. Unfortunately the French and native warriors chose to remain hidden in dense underbrush within rifle shot of the fort. It was July 4th, 1754 when Washington's men took punishing fire from native marksmen behind the protection of the trees. The conflict was halted when a intense July thunderstorm soaked the powder cartouches that silenced the musket fire on both sides. Washington's men promptly broke into the stores of rum and got drunk. A parley was called by the French. Realizing the helplessness of his situation, Washington agreed to a French capitulation proposal, thereby surrendering the little garrison. Unknown to George, he had signed his own confession. Under flickering candlelight in the continuous rainstorm coupled by a confusing translation from French to English, George signed a capitulation agreement which included an admission to the May 25th murder of Ens. Jumonville. The instigator, Tanacharison silently slipped away into the tall forest before the fight began, not to be heard from again during the ensuing French and Indian War. It is said that revengeful wrath knows no bounds. Perhaps it was far too true for Tanacharison for when the signed article of capitulation reached France, war was declared against the British Empire.

With the hostilities underway, British General Braddock returned to seize Fort Duquesne from the French leading some of the King's finest light troops. After crossing the Monogahela River the Highlanders were met by withering fire from a much smaller but well concealed French troops and Native warriors The unexpected loss by such well seasoned troops sent a tacit message to the colonists that the Brits could be beat by inexperienced troops firing rifles from behind trees. All of the British officers were killed and Braddock was mortally wounded, some say by one of his own men. Washington survived unscathed. He had 2 horses shot out from under him and 4 bullet holes in his coat. Being the last officer standing, he arranged an orderly retreat carrying the mortally wounded Braddock back to the Great Meadows.

The following is from a letter written by George Washington to his brother after the battle;

> *By the all-powerful dispensations of Providence, I have been protected beyond all human probability or expectation; for I had four bullets through my coat, and two horses shot under me, yet [I] escaped unhurt, although death was leveling my companions on every side of me!* [20]

In 1758, British General John Forbes, along with Colonel George Washington and Col. Bouquet cut a road through the dense forests of western Pennsylvania erecting forts every 20 miles. The expedition ended at a fort along the banks of the Loyanhanna, some 40 miles from the French built Fort Duquesne. On October 12, 1758, the newly built fort was attacked by the French and their Indian allies. While the British and Virginia forces repelled the attack, they lost all of the livestock outside the fort to the enemies. When Washington arrived with fresh supplies and livestock Forbes ordered his men to prepare to spend the winter in camp and postponed the campaign until spring. One month after the unsuccessful assault on the fort, the French and Indians were planning another attack on the fort. In an attempt to save the horses and cattle from plunder, a company of Virginians under the command of Colonel Mercer, encountered the approaching enemies well away from the walls of the fort. With an afternoon of hot firing, General Forbes ordered Col. Washington to attack th exposed flank of the french position. In the gathering darkness of lthe evening amonst the smoke and fog of war, the two Virginian companies mistook each other and many soldiers died in the friendly fire exchanges. Washington survive by ordering a halt to the firing of his force. Three captives were interrogated when it was learned that the French were in dire straits in their fort. With this information, Forbes ordered Washington to mount an assault over land. As Washington's men approached the fort they were greeted by the sound of a distant explosion. The native warriors with the French had abandon the garrison to return to their families for the coming winter. Realizing their plight the French chose to destroy

Fort Duquesne with explosive effect. When Washington arrived, the last of the French soldiers were paddling their canoes down the Ohio. The war in western Virginia had finally ended, but the broader conflict waged on to the four corners of the world.

When the hostilities finally ceased in 1763, the impact of the French and Indian War was profound. Both combatant countries were in financial ruins. The French had borrowed their way though the conflict, eventually passing it on as high taxes on the landowners and wealthy. The financial mess became one of the many causes of the French Revolution. The British plan to retire their war debts and to continuously funding British soldiers who were placed into the colonists' homes to protect them from Indian raids. The Members of the English Parliament justifiably determined to make the American colonies foot the bill by levying a series of laws and taxes. To the colonists, these actions were viewed as punitive and were soundly rejected as taxation without representation and an invasion of their privacy by the forced quartering of strange soldiers in their homes. The acts of parliament an ocean away set the stage for the next major development in American liberty.

Photo credit to Vivian Ohs, Johnstown, PA

CHAPTER 6. THE FOUNDING OF THE REPUBLIC.

While a number of early American observers claim the foundations of our liberty were erected with the mortar of intense academic debate marked by moments of genius, the cornerstones were actually laid by a highly unlikely group of persecuted outcasts. The genuine founders of the uniquely American form of representative government were originally comprised of a small band of Englishmen bent on shaking off the teachings and authority of the Church of England. Having armed themselves with the bold authority of their faith in the Holy Bible, these hardy pioneers wanted to be liberated from the laws of men while subject only to their God. They became known as Separatists because they were dedicated to separating themselves not only from the English Church but also from England itself.

After having faced severe persecution in their homeland, they fled to Holland where they founded a community of where they could freely exercised their religion. As a cloistered group they developed their own sense of community around their beliefs. The Dutch Government had left them alone, but before long pressures began to mount. Seeking further refuge from government and to spread the Gospel to the heathens in America, the pilgrims petitioned the King of England to grant them a deed for land in the New World. A charter was eventually issued for them to occupy land in the Crown's Virginia Colony, founded in 1603.

With a land title in hand, 102 missionary explorers set sail on the Mayflower August 5, 1620. Midway across the Atlantic Ocean a violent storm blew the small ship hundreds of miles off their intended course. Finally, after surviving three grueling months at sea, these terrified, exhausted wayfarers found themselves off the shores of what is now Cape Cod, Massachusetts.

Aware that their Virginia Charter under English law was worthless on these shores, the undaunted colonists-to-be decided to organize themselves under a written agreement of self-government. The terms they designed while still on their tiny ship became their law; the Mayflower Compact. Being set free of English laws, the pilgrims chose to govern their affairs by their own written covenant. In effect, government by the consent of the governed. The Mayflower Compact became the first legal document of representative government in America. It is as follows;

> *Having undertaken, for the glory of God and the advancement of the Christian Faith and honor of our King and country, a voyage to plant the first colony in the Northern parts of Virginia, do by these presents solemnly and mutually in the presence of God and one another, covenant and combine ourselves together in a civic body politic, for our better ordering and preservation and furtherance of the ends aforesaid, and by virtue hereof to enact, constitute and frame such just law and equal laws, ordinances, acts, constitutions and offices from time to time, as shall be thought most meet and convenient for the general good of the colony. Unto which we promise all due submission and obedience.* [21]

It is one thing to compose idealistic pronouncements about civil government, but quite another matter to test the Compact in the fires of extreme physical hardship and obvious differences of opinions. Time would prove the document held up rather remarkably in spite of the ravages of near starvation, exposure to the elements and arguments that inevitably erupted among the colonists during those most difficult times. The tenets of the Compact prevailed not on the shoulders of physical might but by a commonly shared spirit of cooperation and a deep personal faith in God.

In the absence of their unshakable faith in God's governmental wisdom, it is conceivable this country could have readily fallen under the oppressive political patterns that were characteristic of European governments. In place of the oppressive European models for governance, the Mayflower Compact provided the example for other written constitutions that were based on the consensus of the governed as a foundation of secular law. The law for personal liberty under a representative government, had been birthed in the hearts and minds of the pilgrims on that 11th day of November 1620.

The last chapter noted England's large debt remaining from the successful conclusion of the French and Indian war. Before the conflict, the debt was 72 million pounds. After the war, it rose to 132 million pounds. King George III and his Members of Parliament arrogantly decided to levy a series of heavy taxes onto the colonies. The reaction was predictable. The counter reaction was even more predictable when the Throne added punitive restrictions on top of the taxes. These acts were collectively called the Intolerable Acts. [22]

When might becomes right, the people groan in bondage.

The birth of our American political liberty came as a result of the colonists fierce opposition to the tyrannical rule of King George of England. In political circles, nothing is so loathsome as the arbitrary use of power in order to force a disadvantage people into subjugation. When service to the British rule became overburdening, personal liberty began to take root as a political alternative. As the demands of the Crown increased, the colonists rebelled. And the more the colonists resisted, the more oppressive the King's rule became. It was only a matter of time before the final straw was reached. In March 1770, armed conflict had been avoided, but a unruly crowd of Boston's antagonists, pelted a small guard of British soldiers with snowballs containing rocks and pieces of bricks. The soldiers withdrew defensively into corner, but a soldier fell discharging his musket. A voice in the crowd yelled "fire" and the detachment released a deadly volley into the crowd. Although the soldiers were tried for the accusation of murder, noted Boston attorney John Adams, successfully defended the soldiers actions on the grounds of self defense. The incident became widely known as the Boston massacre when Samuel Adams convinced Paul Revere to memorialize the event with an engraved silver printing plate that showed the soldiers as cold blooded killers. Printed copies of Revere's work became a false but effective political tool to fan the flames of discontent in the colonies. [23]

By 1773, all of the onerous taxes were removed except one, a tax on tea. A British monopoly on tea promised significant revenues since everyone drank tea. The solution provoked the populace even further. Local agitans, called the Sons of Liberty, disguised as Natives stormed British ships in Boston Harbor. They broke open chests of tea and dumped the cargos into the water. The method was replicated as other tea parties occurred in harbors of New York, Annapolis, Philadelphia and distant Charleston, South Carolina. [24]

Representatives of 12 of the 13 colonies met in Philadelphia in September of 1774 to convene the First Continental Congress. Their purpose was to formally petition the British Parliament for redress against the Intolerable acts. They also agreed to boycott British imports. The representatives were to meet for a Second Continental Congress the next year if their objections to the Acts were ignored. Needless to say, the petitions were refused by the Crown.

The colonists began to organized armed resistance to the ever growing presence of British troops in Boston. The volunteers were men ready to respond in a minutes notice to take up arms. Although these minutemen were not planning to strike the first blow, the escalating tensions assured that conflict was inevitable. The precipitating event has been memorialized in prose by Henry Wadsworth Longfellow;

> *Listen my children and you shall hear*
> *Of the midnight ride of Paul Revere,*
> *On the eighteenth of April, in Seventy-five;*
> *Hardly a man is now alive*
> *Who remembers that famous day and year.*
>
> *He said to his friend, "If the British march*
> *By land or sea from the town to-night,*
> *Hang a lantern aloft in the belfry arch*
> *Of the North Church tower as a signal light,--*
> *One if by land, and two if by sea;*
> *And I on the opposite shore will be,*
> *Ready to ride and spread the alarm*
> *Through every Middlesex village and farm,*
> *For the country folk to be up and to arm."*
>
> [25]

On April 19, 1775, the inevitable showdown unfolded in the Lexington, Massachusetts on an open field in front of the town's church. The local minutemen drew a defensive line on the green exposing their lives to the muskets of the most powerful army in the world. When a British officer shouted *"Lay down your arms, you damned rebels, or you are all dead men. Fire!"* the soldiers unleashed a deadly volley killing several brave men. The minutemen scattered into the surrounding woods in confusion, returning sporadic fire. [26]

The British force moved on to Concord were they had planned to seize guns and powder from the town's armory. With word of the Lexington exchange traveling quickly to the Concord minutemen, the locals gathered at the end of a narrow bridge waiting for the British column to arrive. Seeing the bridge blocked by minutemen, the Brits opened fire again.

> By the rude bridge that arched the flood,
> Their flag to April's breeze unfurled,
> Here once the embattled farmers stood
> And fired the shot heard round the world.

Concord Hymn by Ralph Waldo Emerson (1803 -1882)

American blood had been first drawn by British muskets, but return fire from the minutemen caused the Redcoats to withdraw. The ensuing running skirmish drove the soldiers back to the safety of Boston's garrisons. Word traveled quickly across the colonies stirring fiery debates and a general call to arms. With the sides drawn, war was unofficially declared on England.

Following the action on Lexington's green, men put their thoughts to written words deploring the senseless murder of Massachusetts minutemen. The first declaration of independence was approved on May 16, 1775 as the Hannastown Resolve at a small fortification in the back woods of Pennsylvania. The stockade was built along the military road cut out of the wilderness by Col. George Washington under orders by General John Forbes to attack the French Fort Duquesne in 1758. Four days and hundred of miles away, another declaration came out as the Mecklenburg Resolution in North Carolina on May 20,1775. Eventually nearly every county and town in all of the 13 colonies drew up their own sacred American scriptures of independence.

It was in a rather typical historical pattern that the arbitrary rule of a minority stirred the oppressed majority to revolt. Yet, in a very atypical fashion the American war for Independence succeeded to produce a entirely different government that other previous revolutions had. It produced a constitutional republic.

To understand the difference between the American war for independence and other political revolutions one must look closely at the ideals that were precious to those early Americans. First and foremost is the fact that these Americans were entrepreneurs. Recall that many were cast out of Europe for a variety of reasons. The colonist were often considered to be of lower stock than their European counterparts. So it was easy for the English king to rationalize governmental policies that placed the them under his rigid control. King George III truly believed that the New England communities would not nor could not survive without the help of Great Britain. Although this may appeared to have been true, these outcasts had learned to rely on their abilities and their faith rather than England. The rigors of the early colonial experience had also taught them to believe that the hand of Providence was in their favor.

Consider that only a hand full of early Americans could have been educated in such matters as political theory, yet they instinctively recognized the value of personal liberty. Their daily struggles with the harsh environment of a sparsely inhabited land could not be encumbered by regulations. Since they resisted the Crown they were no longer Englishmen. So they became bound by together as Americans for survival against the strongest military force in the world.

When right is might, the people are free.

The personal liberty we all enjoy today in America was paid in full with a great deal of blood, sweat and treasure. A careful examination of the words spoken by one of America's great libertarian and statesmen Patrick Henry speaking before the Virginia House of Burgesses, March 23, 1775.

There is no longer room for hope. If we wish to be free, we must fight! An appeal to arms and to the God of Hosts is all that is left us!

They tell me that we are weak, but shall we gather strength by irresolution? Three million people, armed in the holy cause of liberty and in such a country, are invincible by any force which our enemy can

send against us. We shall not fight alone. God presides over the destinies of nations, and will raise up friends for us. The battle is not to the strong alone; it is to the vigilant, the active, the brave...

Is life so dear, or peace so sweet, as to be purchased at the price of chains and slavery? Forbid it, almighty God! I know not what course others may take, but as for me, give me liberty or give me death!

Other writers of the time embraced the same ideas including William Blackstone, the founder of English common law and John Locke's "Second Treatise on Government", who would provide some of the tools for the political minds of the young country to ponder. However the most influential writing on the development of liberty in America was <u>Common Sense</u> by Thomas Paine in January, 1776. The small booklet provided all the necessary logic for rebellion using the moral authority of the Bible. The pamphlet also called for an immediate declaration of independence from England. Paine's book became a best seller with over 1 million copies sold in America alone. <u>Common Sense</u> unknowingly captured the sentiments of the day and focused the random anger and emotions of the colonists into a laser sharp determination. The contribution to our liberty today is priceless. [27]

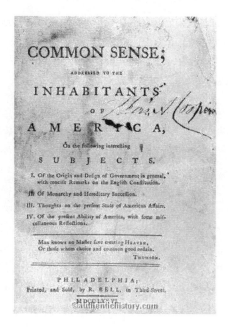

By July 1776, virtually every city and town in the colonies had written separate declarations against England. The collective thoughts towards liberty were eventually captured by Thomas Jefferson in the Declaration of Independence. Those sacred words describing an individual's right to life, liberty and the pursuit of happiness came alive in the hearts of all Americans who longed to be free from Great Britain's tyrannical rule. The radical political announcement to the entire world about the Declaration came as a natural development from centuries of accumulated thought, writings, study and discussion. Although the event was widely heralded as a testament to the genius of Jefferson, it was in reality, the final application of the prevailing sentiments of the day.

In Congress, July 4 1776
The unanimous Declaration of the thirteen united States of America

> *When in the Course of human events, it becomes necessary for one people to dissolve the political bands which have connected them with another, and to assume among the powers of the earth, the separate and equal*

station to which the Laws of Nature and of Nature's God entitle them, a decent respect to the opinions of mankind requires that they should declare the causes which impel them to the separation.

We hold these truths to be self-evident, that all men are created equal, that they are endowed by their Creator with certain unalienable Rights. Among these are Life, Liberty and the pursuit of Happiness — That to secure these rights, Governments are instituted among Men, deriving their just powers from the consent of the governed, — That whenever any Form of Government becomes destructive of these ends, it is the Right of the People to alter or to abolish it, and to institute new Government, laying its foundation on such principles and organizing its powers in such form, as to them shall seem most likely to effect their Safety and Happiness. Prudence, indeed, will dictate that Governments long established should not be changed for light and transient causes; and accordingly all experience hath shewn that mankind are more disposed to suffer, while evils are sufferable than to right themselves by abolishing the forms to which they are accustomed. But when a long train of abuses and usurpations, pursuing invariably the same Object evinces a design to reduce them under absolute Despotism, it is their right, it is their duty, to throw off such Government, and to provide new Guards for their future security. — Such has been the patient sufferance of these Colonies; and such is now the necessity which constrains them to alter their former Systems of Government. The history of the present King of Great Britain is a history of repeated injuries and usurpations, all having

*in direct object the establishment of an absolute
Tyranny over these States. To prove this, let Facts
be submitted to a candid world.......*

The Declaration concluded with the following passage;

*"With a firm reliance on the Divine Providence, we
mutually pledge to each other our lives, our fortunes, and
our sacred honor."* [28]

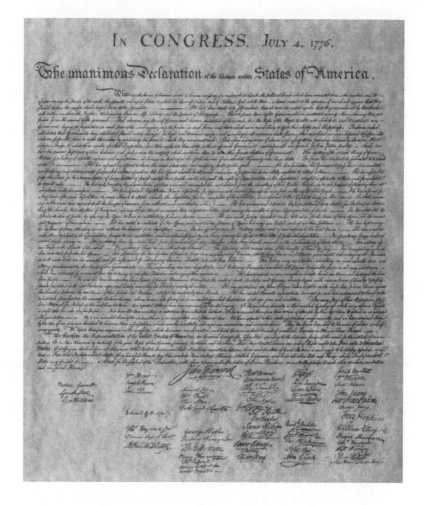

This very Declaration of Independence became the promise for
freedom and liberty for the entire world. The brave men who signed
this historical Declaration of Independence were not wide-eyed

radicals, bent on destruction and anarchy, but men of education, wealth and means who were prepared to give up all they had for rights as free men.

Indeed, as it turned out, being associated with the document carried with it a high price if not a death warrant. Of the 56 signers, five were captured, tortured and killed by the British, twelve lost their homes to looting and burnings and two lost their only sons to the war. In the ensuing war, a total of nine of the original 56 signers gave their lives for the great promise.

The effect was nevertheless the most astounding to the world. With the firm conviction for liberty set in their hearts, the new world colonists would defeat the most powerful nation on earth. It was the American's carefully reasoned commitment to either live free or die which finally triumphed over the British false promises of security for their lives and property. They would bravely and successfully defended their declaration of independence on the field of battle.

Yet, in spite of all the personal and collective sacrifice, only 1 out of 5 colonists fully supported the "holy cause of liberty," while two out of 5 continued their loyalty to the king. The remaining 40 percent passively chose neutrality. Apparently, apathy for the American cause has always been a problem. Four years would pass after the signing of the Declaration of Independence until the dream of a government for the people and of the people was transformed into a binding, legal reality; our first constitution, the Articles of Confederation. [29]

The Second Continental Congress which crafted the Declaration had also been working on Articles of Confederation which would be America's first constitution. Sent to the 13 States in November, 1777 it was not fully ratified by all of the states until March 1781.

> *Articles of Confederation and Perpetual Union Between the States of New Hampshire, Massachusetts Bay, Rhode Island and Providence Plantations, Connecticut, New York, New Jersey, Pennsylvania, Delaware, Maryland, Virginia, North Carolina, South Carolina and Georgia.*

The agreements to a "perpetual union" would be later referenced by Abraham Lincoln as a legal basis of action against the succession of the southern states in 1860.

The American revolutionary war settled the matter after the surrendering of General Cornwall is at Yorktown in October 1781. The Treaty of Paris in 1783, acknowledged the new republic and its lands south of Canada, north of Florida and east of the Mississippi river. Although it was an incredible undertaking costing the lives of over 4400 killed in action and more than 10,000 casualties of war. Far more deaths were caused by sickness and exposure to the elements. Although the history of the war is breathtaking in its entirety, it is not the intent of this book to discuss it in depth. [30] [31]

Following a particularly hot Philadelphia summer in 1787, delegates from the 13 colonies gradually came to agree on the Articles of the Constitution for this new nation; The United States of America. Although many people contributed to the overall framework of the constitution. One man's wisdom stands out as particular witness to the uncertainty of political power. Often referred to as the "father of the Constitution", James Madison revealed his keen insight into the nature of people when he noted; *"If men were angels, no government would be necessary."* Madison's comments reflected the description of man's fallen nature as described in Jeremiah 17. He felt that the natural tendency of man would be to attempt to develop a tyrannical government, thus only the careful scrutiny of men checking the power over men, could prevent tyranny. This idea grew into our system the checks and balances over political power. Madison later wrote, *"No political truth is certainly of greater intrinsic value or is stamped with the authority of more enlightened patrons of liberty than that on which the objection is founded."*

September 17, 1787 marks the day when this document was signed by representatives of the colonies, insuring that promises of the Declaration of Independence would be administered by a government with three separate sources of authority, the executive, the legislative and the judiciary. Not surprisingly, the idea for the three branches of government came from the Biblical passage contained in Isaiah 33:22. "For the Lord is our Judge, the Lord is our lawgiver, the Lord is our King." It is not surprising that the battle cry for the War for Independence was; *"No king but King Jesus"*.

These three separate governmental functions would held accountable to the wisdom and sovereignty of the slow-to-change constitution and the expressions of a majority of the voting populace. Nevertheless, two more years would elapse before the Constitution would be ratified by the individual States.

Unanimously selected to preside over the Constitutional convention, George Washington, who remained relatively quiet until the final hours of formulation, ominously cautioned,

> *"Should the States reject this excellent Constitution, the probability is that an opportunity will never again offer to cancel another in peace-the next will be drawn in blood."*

On the occasion of completing this momentous work, Benjamin Franklin was asked, *"What have you wrought?"* His answer was addressed directly to the point; *"...a Republic, if you can keep it."*

John Adams commented, *"Our Constitution was designed only for a moral and religious people. It is wholly inadequate for the government of any other."*

On another occasion, Washington stated, *"We have raised a standard to which the good and the wise can repair; the event is in the hands of God."*

He would also later write;

> *"The preservation of the sacred fire of liberty and the destiny of the republican model of government, are justly considered, as deeply, perhaps as finally staked, on the experiment intrusted to the hands of the American people."*

During the two years after the signing and the states' final ratification, there was much discussion among the people about this new form of national government. James Madison, along with Alexander Hamilton and John Jay, wrote a series of articles for the people of New York to explain the reasonableness of the federal constitution. The letters to the editor were anonymously signed Publius and became known as the Federalist papers. [32]

Madison explained his ideas in Federalist No. 14.

> *It is, that in a democracy, the people meet and exercise the government in person; in a republic they assemble and administer it by their representatives and agents. A democracy consequently will be confined to a small spot. A republic may be extended over a large region.*

He later also wrote in Federalist 39.

> *If we resort for a criterion, to the different principles on which different forms of government are established, we may define a republic to be, or at least may bestow that name on, a government which derives its powers directly or indirectly from the great body of people; and is administered by persons holding their offices during pleasure, for a limited period. It is essential to such a government that it be derived from the great body of the society...*

The Preamble to the Constitution reveals how this unique document of freedom aptly describes our national purpose: *When right is might the people are free.*

> *We the people of the United States, in Order to form a more perfect Union, establish Justice, insure domestic Tranquility, provide for the common defence, promote the general Welfare, and secure the Blessings of Liberty to ourselves and our Posterity, do ordain and establish this Constitution of the United States of America.*

The following image of a "Signed Copy of the Constitution of the United States; Miscellaneous Papers of the Continental Congress, 1774-1789; Records of the Continental and Confederation Congresses and the Constitutional Convention, 1774-1789, Record Group 360; National Archives." is used with permission as part of the public domain. [33]

The main body of this document contains seven articles that provide for our government's structure:

Article 1 established the Congress which would consist of the House of Representatives and the Senate, determined the eligibility of the voters. It also established our national currency by providing to "... coin money, emit Bills of Credit, make any Thing but gold and silver coin a Tender in Payment of Debts,...".

Article 2 defined the executive branch in the office of the President and Vice-President.

Article 3 created the Judiciary more commonly known as the system of Courts and their jurisdiction.

Article 4 relates to the uniform rights and privileges of citizenship among the States. It also guaranteed the States "...in this Union a Republican Form of Government, and shall protect each of them against Invasion; and...against domestic Violence.

Article 5 provided for amending the Constitution by proposals from either 2/3rds of both Houses OR by 2/3rds of the State Legislatures. Ratification would require 3/4 of the state legislatures to become law. This is the same process that established the original constitution.

Article 6 dealt with the retirement of past debts and the requirement for the officials to be bound by Oath to support the Constitution, and no religious test for qualification to office..

Article 7 required ratification by at least 9 of the 13 states for the establishment of the Constitution as a binding law of the land.

The United States of America, a nation founded on the premise that its supreme political power rests in the collective wisdom of its citizens as expressed through the ballot. By virtue of the citizen's direct consent, the powers of government are granted to elected representatives to carry forth the interests of their constituents within the framework of the Constitution. Not by the whims of a simple majority, but rather within the security of the country's unwavering constitution as upheld by the Supreme Court as noted in 1835 by Alexis de Tocqueville in this quote;

> *The peace, the prosperity, and the very existence of the Union are vested in the hands of the justices of the Supreme Court. Without them, the Constitution would be a dead letter: the executive appeals to them for assistance against the encroachments of the legislative power; the legislature demands their protection against the assaults of the executive; they defend the Union*

from the disobedience of the states, the states from the exaggerated claims of the Union; the public interest against private interests, and the conservative spirit of stability against the fickleness of the democracy.

When right is might, the people are free.

CHAPTER 7. OUR NEW NATION.

The Constitution of the United States became official June 21, 1788, when New Hampshire registered as the ninth state to adopt the document as law, as did Virginia and New York shortly thereafter. However, a number of shortcomings and omissions in the final document opened the door to abuses of the government's powers which could lead to political tyranny. We should recall that it was the arbitrary and tyrannical rule of England's king that compelled America's patriots to fight for America's liberation.

Thomas Jefferson, who was serving as our Ambassador to France during the Constitutional convention, took exception to two elements of our Constitution, which he was generally pleased with. This intrepid defender of liberty was concerned that there were no limitations on the number of terms the president could serve and the lack of sufficient safeguards for the citizen's personal freedom. Jefferson believed that limiting a president's terms of office would protect the government from suffering under the dreaded rule of another tyrant. Additionally, a statement of citizen rights would be needed to protect the citizen from the oppressive rule of a tyrannical government.

It remains clear to us the founding fathers sought to prevent any simple minority from permanently controlling our government, however, another 162 years would pass until the President's terms of the office would be limited.

The first U.S. Congress met March 4, 1789 in New York City, with the result that General George Washington was inaugurated our first President April 30, 1789. Shortly thereafter James Madison presented The Bill of Rights to the House of Representatives. [34]

The preamble to the Bill of Rights is as follows;

> *THE Conventions of a number of the States having at the time of their adopting the Constitution, expressed a desire, in order to prevent misconstruction or abuse of its powers, that further declaratory and restrictive clauses should be added: And as extending the ground of public confidence in the Government, will best insure the beneficent ends of its institution*
>
> *RESOLVED by the Senate and House of Representatives of the United States of America, in Congress assembled, two thirds of both Houses concurring, that the following Articles be proposed to the Legislatures of the several States, as Amendments to the Constitution of the United States, all or any of which Articles, when ratified by three fourths of the said Legislatures, to be valid to all intents and purposes, as part of the said Constitution; viz.:*
>
> *ARTICLES in addition to, and Amendment of the Constitution of the United States of America, proposed by Congress, and ratified by the Legislatures of the several States, pursuant to the fifth Article of the original Constitution.*

Amendment I (original)

> *Congress shall make no law respecting an establishing of religion, or prohibiting the free exercise thereof; or abridging the freedom of speech, or of the press, or the right of the people peaceable to assemble, and to petition the Government for a redress of grievances.*

We can appreciate in this Amendment the intention to prevent our Government from establishing a religion as had been done with King Henry's Church of England. Furthermore, the free exercise of religion meant the freedom of conscience regardless of religious or doctrinal affiliations. Morality was encouraged at this time in history and efforts were not made to interfere in religious expression or worship. The best example of the Founder's attitude toward religion in America can be found in the first official matter of business after the Constitution was ratified. The very first Act of Congress authorized the printing, at the government's expense, of 20,000 Bibles to be distributed to the "heathen" natives. Prior to this time, British law prohibited the publishing of an Bible in the English language on American soil. Clearly the English Parliament understood the political power of the Word .

Notice that the clause, "separation of church and state", is not included in the first amendment. This popular but constitutionally false statement was lifted from a personal letter from President Thomas Jefferson to the Danbury Baptist Association. The entire quotation takes on a totally different light when it is reviewed in its proper context.

> *Believing with you that religion is a matter lies solely between man and his God; that he owes account to none other for his faith or his worship; that the legislative powers of the government reach actions only, and not opinions, -- I contemplate with sovereign reverence that act of the whole American people which declare that their legislature should "make no law respecting an establishment of religion or prohibiting the free exercise thereof," thus building a wall of separation between church and state.*

Clearly, this private quotation was not intended to deny religious people a special favor that is not offered to the general public! Sadly, today this quotation is often being used to discriminate against Christian Americans while other non-Christian religious groups are protected. Obviously, the influence of Christianity in our government is well founded in our early roots. The vast majority of the founders insisted that our government would succeed only if its laws reflected the "Kingdom of God" on earth.

Other first amendment freedoms, which include speech and a free press have been vigorously defended by our Supreme Court. The right of assembly and to petition the government to solve our problems are yet another American trademark.

Amendment II. (original)

> *A well regulated Militia, being necessary for the security of a free State, the right of the people to keep and bear Arms, shall not be infringed.*

With the fierce hatred for tyrannical rulers deeply planted in their hearts and minds, the founding fathers knew that our national strength is nothing more than the strength of our individuals, whether they be counted collectively as ballots or bullets. Since diversity of the common strength was viewed as the principle purpose supporting our republican form of government, the armed private citizen was therefore "necessary to the security of a free State." Clearly the 2nd Amendment was intended to be a personal right to protect the American citizen and the citizen soldier as necessary for freedom. In 2009, the U.S. Supreme Court affirmed the original intent of this amendment. It still stands today.

Amendment III. (original)

> *No soldier shall, in time of peace be quartered in any house, without the consent of the Owner, nor in time of war, but in a manner to be prescribed by law.*

After the French and Indian war, British soldiers were placed into private homes supposedly to protect them from the raiding bands of Indians when we were no longer at war with them. During the war for America's liberation from England, many colonists were forced to feed and shelter British troops. The experience of the burdening unwilling private citizens with the expenses of provisions and shelter lead to this Amendment.

Amendment IV (condensed)

> *The right of the people to be secure in their persons, houses, papers and effects, against unreasonable searches and seizures...*

The right to privacy is another hallmark of our liberties. Amendment IV further requires written reasons for any government action against a citizen. This amendment again reflects the Founder's concern to prevent tyrannical and arbitrary government and the protection of its citizens from political abuses of power.

Amendment V (condensed)

> *No person could be deprived of their "...life, liberty or property, without due process of law;*

In matters pertaining to the Federal jurisdiction, due process of law meant that an individual was protected from forcible action by the government by judicial procedures which allowed the person to have an impartial trial including the right to an appeal up to the Supreme Court of the United States. This amendment right did not apply the States. Notice that "life, liberty or property reflect the same order of importance and sequence as stated in the Declaration of Independence's " Life, liberty and the pursuit of happiness".

Amendment VI. (condensed)

> *In all criminal prosecutions, the accused shall enjoy the right to a speedy and public trial, by an impartial jury of the State and district wherein the crime shall have been committed....*

This amendment also requires a writ or accusations in writing, a preponderance of evidence, a right to a lawyer, cross-examination of evidence, witnesses, and a trial by an impartial jury.

Amendment VII. (original)

> *In suits at common law, where the value in controversy shall exceed twenty dollars, the right of trial by jury shall be preserved, and no fact tried by a jury, shall be otherwise reexamined in any Court of the United States, than according to the rules of the common law.*

This amendment assured that civil law suits were guaranteed a day in court before an impartial jury, and that the right to an appeal was limited to procedural issues, not the facts of the case.

Amendment VIII. (original)

Excessive bail shall not be required, nor excessive fines imposed, nor cruel and unusual punishment inflicted.

The definition of excessive bail, i.e. a security pledge of money to make sure the accused didn't run off. The definition of cruel and unusual punishments were left to the interpretation of the courts and in some cases been misused by both the judges and the juries.

Amendment IX. (original)

The enumeration in the Constitution, of certain rights, shall not be construed to deny or disparage others retained by the people.

This amendment also formed the basis of an individual's natural right to be able to make individual choices without any federal government interference as long as these choices do not interfere with the rights of others.

Amendment X. (original)

The powers not delegated to the United States by the Constitution, nor prohibited by it to the States, are reserved to the States respectively, or to the people.

The tenth amendment establishes a wall of separation protecting the state rights from unwarranted Federal actions. It also protects the citizens from Federally unconstitutional behavior. In effect, this amendment is the cornerstone of law that was to be a check on the powers of the Federal government.

This Bill of Rights was designed specifically to protect the citizen from the abuses of an oppressive government, as they had been experienced under the heavy hand of Great Britain. These rights are guaranteed by the Federal Constitution can cannot be abridged by federal, state, county, or local government.

These rights, backed by the powers of our national government, are what makes Americans free.

Yet it was another 82 years before anyone had any legal remedy when their civil rights were violated. This act was passed to stop the Ku Klux Klan from using the pretense of "official" activities under the jurisdiction of law, i.e. the "color of the law" to deprive former slaves of their civil rights.

Section 1983 of U.S. Title 42 of the Civil Rights Act of 1871 provides:

> *Every person who, under color of any statute, ordinance, regulation, custom, or usage, of any State or Territory or the District of Columbia, subjects, or causes to be subjected, any citizen of the United States or other person within the jurisdiction thereof to the deprivation of any rights, privileges, or immunities secured by the Constitution and laws, shall be liable to the party injured in an action at law, suit in equity, or other proper proceeding for redress.*

Later the U.S. Supreme Court acknowledged that the "person" applied to all actors in all levels of governments who would to be personally liable for damages.

When right is might, the people are free.

CHAPTER 8. LIBERTY AMENDS
THE CONSTITUTION.

Sixteen amendments have been added to the Constitution since those early days. Some of these amendments directly affirm the founder's protection or extension of personal liberty while other amendments related to procedural matters. Those changes that affected the liberties of Americans will be discussed in this chapter. The 13ᵗʰ Amendment was ratified December 6, 1865;

> *Neither slavery nor involuntary servitude, except as a punishment for crime whereof the party shall have been duly convicted, shall exist within the United States, or any place subject to their jurisdiction.*

When Thomas Jefferson declared the political idea of personal liberty as an inalienable right granted by God to men and women, he intended to exclude no citizen. The Northwest Territories Ordinance of 1878 prohibited slavery in the federal land east of the Mississippi River, north of the Ohio River and south of the Great Lakes. This amendment corrects the constitution which would have rejected by failed ratification of the southern states if slaves were permitted to be counted as citizens instead of property. During the constitutional convention in 1787 a compromise was reached with the southern states that permitted slavery until 1808 at which time all slavery would be abolished in the United States. Tobacco farmers in the south needed skilled labor to handle the profitable weed. A good tobacco worker was worth keeping well. Recognizing their value, land owners treated the slaves and their families as investments in their future profits. Cotton crops were much easier to harvest by virtually anyone who was well enough to take to the fields. When the market demand for cotton increased land owners began to exploit the unskilled labor of slaves of all ages. Simultaneously, the Spanish presence in Florida presented a threat to the southern states. Eventually political pressures from southern legislators ignored the 1808 deadline forcing the issue to be tabled indefinitely. The debate over this unequal standard of rights between free people and slaves was ultimately settled by the Civil War. The failure of our founders to resolve this touchy issue nearly cost us our country! It remained for the 13th Amendment to permanently put the matter to rest.

Amendment XIV. (ratified July 9, 1868)

> *Section 1. All persons born or naturalized in the United States and subject to the jurisdiction thereof, are citizens of the United States wherein they reside. No State shall make or enforce any law which shall abridge the privileges or immunities of citizens of the United States; nor shall any State deprive any person of life, liberty or property, without due process of law; nor deny any person within its jurisdiction the equal protection of the laws.*

In other words, the 14th Amendment extended the personal rights under the federal constitutional over any state rights. In effect, federal rights trumped the states powers to protect American citizens from arbitrary action by state governments. Notice that once again the writers placed life before liberty or property.

Amendment XV. (ratified February 3, 1870)

> *Section 1. The right of the citizens of the United States to vote shall not be denied or abridged by the United States or by any State on account of race, color, or previous condition of servitude.*

Under the provisions of the 15th Amendment, the right to vote had finally been extended to all male citizens who had reached their 21st birthday.

Amendment XVI. (ratified February 3, 1913)

> *The Congress shall have the power to lay and collect taxes on incomes, from whatever source derived, without apportionment among the several States, and without regard to any census or enumeration.*

It was the fear of oppressive taxation from a tyrannical government that prevented this amendment from becoming Constitutional law for some 126 years. This amendment was made in response to the conflicting U.S. Supreme court decisions dating back to the Civil War. Income taxes had been considered to be a direct tax and therefore not subjected to a Federal requirement for the states to share their collections with the Federal Government according to the state's population. This amendment made it legal for the Federal Government to levy taxes on personal income regardless of where they lived. Ratification came under a cloud of deception which is still in question over 100 years later.

Seen as a success for the fledgling progressive movement, the 16th Amendment was promoted with the express "promise" that these income taxes would NEVER exceed 7% on the highest incomes and 1% on the rest of the people. Keeping to character of America's first progressive in chief, President Woodrow Wilson, the tax rates sky rocketed during the war to end all wars, WWI. To the mutual sadness and frustration of us all, the federal income tax has progressively burdened successful Americans forcing them to share their wealth with others. We continue to struggle under this hopelessly complicated social tool of the progressives under the guise of "social justice. None of which was the understanding of the American people when the amendment was ratified. Progressives view it as a method to make our country perfect whether Americans agree to the terms of perfection or not.

Amendment XVII. Ratified April 8, 1913, it modified Article 1, section 3 of the Constitution.

The Senate of the United States shall be composed of two Senators from each State, elected by the people thereof, for six years; and each Senator shall have one vote. The electors in each State shall have the qualifications requisite for electors of the most numerous branch of the State legislatures.

Our founding fathers knew of the potential of dangers associated with totally open democracies. A mob mentality at the ballot box could create a tyrant. Without some check and balance on the whims of public sentiments, our republic could fall into the wrong hands. Article 1, section 3 of the Constitution was part of the original intent to prevent such a mob rule from gaining power in the Federal government. The process of selecting Senators by the legislators of the states was seen as way to allow the interests of the states to participate in Congress. It was seen as a way to stabilize the government from any radical changes in the House of Representatives or the Presidency. However the leaders of the early Progressive movement knew that the best way to advance their socialist agenda would be by the direct election of U. S. Senators. They knew that this amendment would allow them to gain greater control of the Senate and its power. This amendment was a serious mistake and should be repealed to protect the states rights in the tenth amendment.

Amendment XVIII condensed (ratified January 16, 1919)
Section 1.

After one year from the ratification of this article the manufacture, sale, or transportation of intoxicating liquors within, the importation thereof into, or the exportation thereof from the United States and all territory subject to the jurisdiction thereof for beverage purposes is hereby prohibited.

The 18th amendment banned the manufacture, sale or transportation of alcoholic beverages in the United States. It did not prohibited an individual from privately consuming alcoholic beverages. The unenforceable nature of this law soon became obvious. It simply drove the all of the alcohol sales underground into the black market. When government attempted to discourage personal consumption by adding poison to the booze to denatured the alcohol, many people unknowingly drank it and died. Many historians feel that this amendment created the atmosphere for organized crime. Others argues for legalizing alcohol because it could be a source of tax revenues. It wasn't long before the amendment was repealed in 1933 by the 21st Amendment. It stands as a reminder that the abuses of alcohol had become a significant national problem and that taxes derived from any source would be happily received by government..

Amendment XIX. (ratified August 18, 1920)

> *The right of the citizens of the United States to vote shall not be denied or abridged by the United States or by any State on account of sex.*

Rights for women took a giant step forward with the passing of this Amendment! We can only guess about the ways our early history might have been if nearly one half of the population had been permitted to vote from the very beginning.

Amendment XXII. condensed (ratified February 27, 1951)

> Section 1. No person shall be elected to the office of the President more than twice,...

This amendment was a direct result of Franklin Roosevelt's attempt to become a President for life. Never before in the history of our republic would anyone ever succeed in becoming a monarch over our government. FDR got close to becoming the first American king. All of the previous presidents were either not re-elected or declined to run beyond a second term of office out of respect to our historical dislike of political tyrants. Yet, FDR was elected and re-elected three more times to the office of president.

Unfortunately for Americans, he also succeeded in changing the undermining philosophy of American government. FDR continued the progressive agenda to create a large proactive Federal government. This progressive shift towards socialism forever changed the direction of our government while establishing a permanent dependant class of Americans. The clever lies hidden in FDR's messages ensured his re-election because he knew that people would vote for politicians who offered the voters a free lunch. His administration proved that "power tends to corrupt, absolute power corrupts absolutely". The entire nation realized the grave danger of imperial presidencies when this amendment was approved.

Amendment XXIV. (ratified January 23, 1964)

> *The right of citizens of the United States to vote in any primary or other election for President or Vice President, or for Senator or Representative in Congress, shall not be denied or abridged by the United States or any State by reason of failure to pay any poll tax or other tax.*

I find it sometimes hard to imagine that voters had to pay a poll tax to vote. Yet this kind of political trickery actually took place in our country as recently as the 1960s. It was being used as tool to prevent blacks from voting. The practice of paying to vote must have been widespread in order to require a constitutional amendment to ban the practice.

Amendment XXVI. (ratified July 1, 1971)

> *Section 1. The right of citizens of the United States, who are eighteen years of age or older, to vote shall not be denied or abridged by the United States or by any State on account of age.*

A by product of the Vietnam War, this Amendment was passed to allow more voters to participate in elections. Soldiers under the age of 21 were old enough to kill and possibly be killed in armed conflict on behalf of their country, but not old enough to vote. Progressive radicals in colleges and universities pushed for the amendment as a tool of empowerment for themselves against the "Establishment". Their mantra was "Don't trust anyone over 30". The radicals' intentions became obvious when a mob of young political activists demonstrating outside the 1972 Democratic National Convention turned it into a violent confrontation. The protests of the radical progressives caused our military to withdraw from Viet Nam in 1975 just when victory was certain. The founders intent of preventing radicals from seizing control of government was sadly ignored for they knew that youth does not always equate with wisdom.

Amendment XXVII (proposed by Madison in 1789 ratified in 1992.)

> *No law, varying the compensation for the services of the Senators and Representatives, shall take effect, until an election of Representatives shall have intervened.*

Imagine that, after 203 years of raising their own salaries, Senators and Congressmen could no longer vote themselves a pay raise. If a salary increase were to be approved, the raise would apply to the following session of Congress. Those members of Congress who wanted an increase would now be held accountable to the ballot box in the next election.

CHAPTER 9. LIBERTY AND THE FEDERAL BUREAUCRACY

What set our forefathers apart from the rest of society during their time was their determination to weave personal liberty into the fabric of every citizen's life. However, the progressive expansion of our Federal Government far beyond the confines of its legitimate functions under the Constitution has rung the death knell of all too many of the basic principles of individual freedom envisioned by our Founding Fathers.

Many years would pass after the initial events of the War of American Independence, the ratification of our Constitution and Bill of Rights before any significant changes to expand individual freedom emerged in the United States of America.

The slavery issue alone served to fracture our great nation by threatening to divide its people forever. But the United States survived the Civil War largely because of our commitment to the Constitutional guarantees of personal freedom and liberty for all citizens. True to the thinking and ideals of the original founders, the ideas of personal liberty had once again proven itself to be more powerful than economic interests. Americans were more willing to risk their lives in order to preserve their liberties than any other cause, including the quest for financial gain in the marketplace or the amassing of property.

The next major threat to our liberties came in 1887 with a

new era of a government; the age of bureaucracy. The birth of the federal bureaucracy occurred with the formation of the first strictly administrative agency, the Interstate Commerce Commission, known today as the I.C.C.. According to the U.S. Constitution, the Federal Government was to have played a very limited role in the affairs of the states and its citizens. The I.C.C. opened the doors into a slightly different direction.

The I.C.C. was created by Congress in an effort to resolve a price dispute between the railroad operators and grain farmers. The issue involved the cost of transporting crops across state lines. The conflict demanded federal involvement since the dispute involved interstate matters. Congress was unwilling to invest time to properly review the large number of complaints. The Supreme Court decision moved Congress to created an agency with limited executive, judicial and legislative authority intended to investigate and ultimately solve the special problems of these conflicting interests. Sadly, for the fate of our individual freedoms and personal liberty, the pattern designed with the formation of the I.C.C. set a precedent that would extend into the future.

From a purely practical standpoint, the I.C.C. appeared to make a lot of sense, however, from a personal liberty viewpoint, handing over the power ultimately exerted by this free standing governmental agency was also a potential threat to the citizen. Although the I.C.C. was designed to be accountable to Congress and the Courts, it also became a model for removal of government's power from the checks and balances of the ballot.

The question that arose in the minds of citizens was; "What can the voter do to modify or restrain the actions of this Commission?" The case presented the classic head-to-head confrontation over the politics of power.

The dilemma revolved around whether government can serve its people when it's no longer directly accountable to the voters as opposed to whether an administrative agency can accomplish its goals when it is "playing politics" at the same time.

On the one hand, the question would be; how can the government get on with its business when every issue must be decided by legislators? On the other, must the voter let everything their ancestors fought for be given to a few appointed career bureaucrats?

In the aftermath of the I.C.C.'s creation, standards were set up by the bureaucrats that would eventually grow into an enormous federal appetite for money. These special interest groups soon realized that if they could convince the commissioners to lean towards their favor, they could steer the power of government to their advantage. The ploy became known as the fox guarding the hen house. The shared political interests developed into an "iron triangle" of power by which the tight control over the administrative power is held by the federal agencies, the special interest lobby and the oversight subcommittees of Congress.

Since 1887, the federal and state governments have used the I.C.C. as a model agency to provide solutions for many other problems of society. With the age of bureaucracy well under way, both the state and federal governments needed more money to operate these agencies. Tariffs and duties imposed on the citizens provided only a small portion of the revenues needed to feed the growing administrative branch of government, but by the early 1900's it became obvious that additional money would be required to insure their survival.

The ratification in the Sixteenth Amendment in 1913 secured the of future progressive government expansion through the leveling of personal income taxes. Eventually, as more federal agencies were added to an ever-expanding government under the disguise of serving the public interest, our bureaucracy in Washington was managing to slowly expand its influence on the lives of all Americans.

When our republican form of government was created, the principal fear expressed by the Founders stemmed from the concern that arbitrary use of power applied on behalf of the interests of a minority of people would put the ruler controlling that power above the interests of the majority and the law itself. To insure such misuse of power or tyrannical rule would be avoided, our Founding Fathers insisted our governmental power would only be exercised whenever it could be applied in the interests of the majority of the people. And that power would, they stressed, be applied by the majority of the people. But with the development of a separate administrative branch of government, bureaucrats could now possess a large measure of the previously separated powers of government, often with little oversight or accountability to Congress. However well intended, poorly designed legislative mandates could only produce bad regulations and programs.

From the creation of the ICC, federal bureaucracies have grown to employ 2.2 million people by 2020 in three separate areas;

1. Independent regulatory agencies that create and enforce rules over the economy.
2. Fifteen cabinet departments each led by presidentially appointed Secretary who must be confirmed by a majority of the Senate. e.g. the Department and Secretary of Defense.
3. Government corporations who compete with the private sector to provide services at prices that are below the market rate. e.g. FannieMae and discount mortgages.

By 2019, salaries for Federal bureaucrats averaged $115,000 each. The private sector average was around $53,400.00. The difference can be attributed to both the unionization of the public sector workers and a political agenda which encourages the progressive expansion of government. Although past legislation protects civil servants from partisan politics, the fact remains that waste, fraud and abuse will most certainly occur when the pressures for performance and thrift in the marketplace are suspended. The most egregious and recent example is the Covid -19 pandemic. Bureaucratic bungling under politically correct pressures from elected politicians undermined the entire world economy while anarchists take over parts of some major cities.

Armed with the tax dollars required to execute their congressional mandates these bureaucrats could, in fact, become petty tyrants. The recent threats by the EPA to regulate global warming instead of Congress legislating the issue is the latest example. Here the EPA appears to be more like a teenager threatening his parent, the Congress of the United States.

Today people are becoming enslaved into political correctness by the very slow but progressive expansion of the 4th branch of

Government, the Federal Bureaucracy. James Madison warned about this in the following quotation;

> *I believe there are more instances of the abridgement of the freedom of the people by the gradual and silent encroachments of those in power than by violent and sudden usurpations.*

CHAPTER 10. THE
ECONOMICS OF LIBERTY.

Few people realize how the American capitalist economy was started. The true beginnings of our historically unique money system was founded in the Plymouth colony in Massachusetts. Remember that the European system of money and property placed the ownership of most of the property into the hands of feudal lords and the money under the control of the kings.

History has shown that human nature tends towards apathy unless there is a motivation for rewards. However, the work ethic can become confused even amongst a pious group such as the pilgrims in the Plymouth colony in 1621. In the first growing season, the commune approach to raising crops in a common field that all were expected to work failed to produce the needed supply. By the second winter, food had once again become scarce. Pain from hunger is a powerful motivation to avoid the a similar experience. Realizing that the struggling colony could fail without an adequate surplus of food, the colony's Governor William Bradford, came upon a unique solution. Each colonist was given a seven acre tract of land, with multiples of seven for each family member. In exchange for this private ownership of property. The colonists were only required to give 10% of their harvests back to the colony storehouse. The Governor then posted the following quotation from the Paul's second letter to the Thessalonians Chapter 3 verse 10; on the door of the community hall. "If anyone will not work, neither shall he eat." The harvest was greater than expected leading to a celebration of the first Thanksgiving in America. In effect, individuals pursing their own interests produce more than the collective interests of a community, even under the most altruistic set of values.

Over the next two centuries people came to America to seek fortunes, escape debtors and poverty. For those who could afford the costs of passage, they could begin a new life anywhere their money and interests could take them. For those yearning to be free but without money, a common ticket was by a contract of indentured servitude. In these cases, an individual agreed to repay for their passage by serving under an existing landowner for a number of years. After the term of obligation ended, they were free to fend for themselves.

The melting pot of the European migration to our country brought a variety of economic habits with them, often including an unwillingness to work. Eventually all newcomers had to find a way to feed, clothe, and shelter themselves. Freed of the ways of the old world, immigrants created their own way of bettering themselves by a simple formula, self preservation under survival of the fittest. As difficult as it would seem, for the first time in their lives, they had an opportunity to buy a piece of the abundant and inexpensive acres of land.

Thus, our unique system of private property and individual responsibility was born. The community standards of the Protestant's work-equals-worth ethic would serve to keep the economy growing and in balance. By helping themselves they produced more than they needed which could be used to trade the surplus for goods that other had in surplus. This was the beginning of the uniquely American version of a free market economy that became known as capitalism. It was this morally based work ethic and the renown Yankee ingenuity that created the intense self-reliance of the American economy that nurtured and sustained the young country during its early history.

As our nation progressed, our famous work ethic expanded the economy beyond the predominantly agricultural economic base to the growing factories and industries. Along with the deep sense of a moral obligation to work for one's daily bread, was the commitment towards staying out of debt. The borrower is the lenders slave and few wanted to be working for the gain of someone else. Business indebtedness was low and government support of private industry was unthinkable. And, of course, if one didn't pay their bills they were quickly sent to the many debtors prisons. There was a very undesirable price for abusing their freedom by mishandling their money.

The great American work ethic began to change with the our Civil War. Like many other wars, the demand for war materials jump-started the economy into what is known as the Industrial Revolution. The sudden demand for large quantities of goods spurred the nation's businesses to develop ways to meet the need of a country at war. The buyers were none other than the opposing governments at war.

After the civil war ended and as the 19th century progressed, bigger business gradually replaced smaller ones. By the end of that century, big business profiteers found that they could abuse the millions of uneducated immigrants who were fleeing the poverty of Europe in search of a better life in America. The blatant abuses soon lead to rebellion against those industrial tyrants. With so much violence, the federal government was eventually called to intervene in these disputes between businesses and labor. *When might is right, the people groan in bondage.*

By the turn of the 20th century, the direction of the government regulators had shifted away from the big bosses towards the workers. Laborers organized into unions and the unions flexed their muscles into the political process. In response to the political activism of the unpin vote, Federal legislation was crafted to end abusive labor policies. Although the laws caused higher labor wages and benefits, the costs were passed on to the consumer through increased prices for finished goods. Business taxes remained relatively low, but business indebtedness began to increase to a small, but sizeable percentage of the cost of doing business.

Enter the 16th amendment and the introduction of Federal income taxes in 1913. While the original tax rate was only 7% for the rich, by the end of the decade and the first world war, the top rate had risen to 73%. The elevated tax rate caused an unexpected result. Federal income tax revenue dropped and the national debt ballooned to $24 billion.

After the allied victory in World War I, America had become a major world power. Our national confidence soared even further when our soldiers returned home. The jubilation carried over into our economic matters as Americans felt secure about their future. President Coolidge spearheaded the lowering of federal income taxes on the rich to 25% between 1921 and 1926 while tax revenues increased three fold. The infusion of increased revenue reduced the national debt to $18 billion.

Private money began to flow back into the economy from the top down with the burden of taxes partially relieved. Amid the great American confidence from military victory in WWI, an unusual period of prosperity emerged. Unemployment fell to 1% and the middle class was born. The era of the economic growth became known as the Roaring Twenties. An astute Secretary of the Treasury, Andrew Mellon observed the relationship between lowering the high tax rates on the wealthy, and the increase of tax revenues flowing into the national treasury. The explanation was simple; rich people have the resources to move their wealth away from investments to avoid onerous taxes. The old adage of the golden rule of money was understandable;"He who has the gold, rules". Not to leave a good thing alone, President Hoover began to spend the surplus with more government programs.

Unfortunately, the euphoria of so much wealth, people became careless about their money habits. Over time the usual conservative Yankee attitude towards money relaxed its guard. The caution was discarded by the lure of get-rich-quick schemes many of which were stimulated by the prohibition of alcoholic beverages. The something-for-nothing attitude became a national pastime particularly with the stock market. Coupled with the investment fever were the credit institutions and banks who were more than willing to loan money to any anybody who held a steady job.

On Wall Street, all went well until that fateful day of reckoning in October of 1929 when the New York Stock Market collapsed. The sudden loss of great wealth shocked the national conscience about the liquidity of wealth. The years of economic foolishness with its unlimited borrowing and spending had ended. The wealth of the fools disappeared overnight. The social cost could be measured in the national unemployment rate as 1 out of every 5 workers were quickly out of a full time job. Payback would be hell indeed for those who believed that they could get something for nothing. People loved capitalism when it was successful, but began to hate it when greed caused economic pain. After the Stock Market Crash of 1929 slammed our industrial base, our national economy was struck with another blow; the dreadful dust bowl days of the 1930s.The period became known as the Great Depression.

In 1889, Congress declared 2 million acres of land in the Oklahoma territory that had been seized from the native tribes to be part of the public domain. Soon after the federal government offered 160 acres of land for free to any willing soul who would settle there. The great land rush of Oklahoma stirred migration from all over the country. By the 1920s, newly mechanized farm equipment made available by advances in assembly line production turned over tens of thousands of acres. The harvest was plentiful until the land dropped into a extended drought in the early 1930s. Years of careless land management left the soil to dry under unrelenting exposure to the hot mid western sun. Valuable topsoil became dust that was easily carried away in the ever present wind. The agriculture sector was devastated causing an alarming increase in the price of food. [35]

In a capitalist economy, setbacks do not mean failure. The risks to achieve success include a risk for loss. The years of economic hardship during the depression spurred a public outcry for political solutions. The conservative view was to allow the economy to self correct. The progressive solution was to inject a massive amount of government money into the economy though stimulus spending programs. The Keynesian theory of progressive economic solution became popularized in the presidential candidacy of Democrat Franklin Delano Roosevelt. He promised Americans a return to prosperity using broadly defined federal programs and lots of borrowed money.

Although these spending programs were largely unconstitutional, Roosevelt's New Deal borrowed from the future and offered the resources of the federal government to soothe the wounds of the fiscal folly and bad weather.

The formation of the I.C.C. in 1887 as well as the introduction of the personal income tax in 1913, set the stage for Big Brother government to step in. The development of this fourth branch of government initiated an enormous step toward the breakdown of our individual liberties. The most rapid growth of bureaucracy came in response to the Great Depression of 1930.

During previous economic down cycles Americans relied upon thrift and hard work to revive their economy. This work ethic permitted a level of personal freedom to grow the troubled economy at a grass roots level. But instead of resorting to the tried and proven methods of wise economic growth on a personal level, the depths of this depression caused voters to seek a quick fix solution by government supposedly without any further financial pain.

After his election, in 1932, FDR's administration pushed his New Deal agenda through the Congress. The Supreme Court immediately objected to the constitutionality of many of his programs because of their clearly socialist nature. In response FDR often used a unethical process of "stonewalling" his social programs into place before the Court could object. By the time that the Court got a chance to review the policy, and quite often rule against it, the program's money was already spent.

The Supreme Court repeatedly ruled against FDR and his economic programs. In another tactic, he attempted to end-run the constitution by expanding the 9 member bench to 12. If he would have succeeded, he could have been able to appoint three new justices who would be sympathetic towards his socialist programs. This idea failed, however over the course of his unprecedented four terms of office, he managed to appoint new justices whenever one of the Justices retired.

FDR also took us off of the constitutionally mandated gold standard. This decision undercut the long range stability of the economy while appearing to help the immediate needs of the poor.

But this previously unconstitutional, (Article I. Section 10.) act opened the door for inflation. The stability of our economic system lay in the slow-to-change quantity of gold reserves that backed up the value of the paper currency. Whenever the gold standard was eliminated, paper money could become whatever value that the government wished to give it. With the creation of the Federal Reserve system in 1913 our money supply came under the control of an independent network of commercial banks, the Federal Reserve. Acting independently of Congress or the President, the Federal Reserve could release more or less credit to the banks at a predetermined interest rate depending on whether they wanted to stimulate or slow the economy.

One may ask; "How could Roosevelt get away with such un-American policies?" By remaining popular with the majority of the voters. American voters began to like the taste of the easy government money which was really nothing more than redistributed tax dollars or borrowed from the future.

In spite of what many will say, FDR did not lift us out of the Great Depression of the 1930s. The Japanese sneak attack on Pearl Harbor in 1941 did. The shock to America, particularly after the victory in World War 1, came like a cold shower. Now Americans had a common enemy that would unite the America economy into action that ended the New Deal mentality.

As so many times in history, the threat to the nation's security produced an avalanche of support and an immediate demand for war materials. The combination of these two forces pushed the economy out of the doldrums. World War II brought us out of the depression, at a cost of deep governmental and business indebtedness. Money that had to be repaid with future taxes.

The Cold War years between 1950 and 1970 saw the greatest expansion of businesses this country has ever seen. The arms race in response to the Soviet and Chinese nuclear threat, the Korean Conflict, the Vietnam War, and finally the space race to the moon were all examples of national security projects that built a huge military industrial economy consuming vast sums of tax dollars and borrowed money. The net effect on the private sector was the creation of jobs and an expanding national economy. Labor costs increased, but so did profits. American products, technology and know-how ruled the world. America had become a super power on the world stage.

The major domestic issues focused on the civil rights and poverty. During the Kennedy and Johnson administrations domestic social programs, such as the "Great Society" were used by the Federal government in an attempt to reverse our nation's sad history of racial discrimination. Civil rights marches and urban violence filled the headlines that spurred the body politic to use the taxpayer's money to solve these social problems. The combined war against poverty and the anti-discrimination programs promised to eradicate poverty and racial prejudice in America. Instead it ushered in an era of wasteful spending and government regulation. Only a small percentage of the allocated money trickled down into the hands of he poor people. Bureaucrats and special interest contractors took the lion's share of the Great Society funds. What was really needed was a deregulated economy with lower taxes which would create job opportunities for those who wanted to better their lives not more handouts that trapped the minorities into a perpetual dependance on government aid.

The social safety nets became hammocks which sustained the dependance class.

On the political front politicians learned that the voters liked the government's handouts. The formula to a permanent career in politics was discovered; give the voters money even if it means borrowing it and you'll stay in power in Washington.

Along with the promises were higher taxes squeezing the budgets of the traditional family unit of a one income household. Today marriage rates are at a 150 year low, not seen since after the civil war when fewer men were available to marry. The introduction of the birth control pill offered women more life choices. Women choose to pursue their own careers during their childbearing years rather than becoming moms to the next generation. The birth rate has plunged to a record low. The legalization of abortion by the Supreme Court decision on Roe v Wade in 1973 became a back up form of birth control that changed the hearts of pregnant women into cold hearted indifference for the life within. Planned Parenthood originally founded to reduce the populations of African-Americans now offers abortion services that focus in the inner cities particularly for the minority population. Currently there are more abortions of black babies in New York City than births. The "freedom" from their monthly cycles and unwanted pregnancies fueled the rise of the feminist movement. Women now had more economic opportunities but it opened up a battleground between the sexes competing for the jobs held by men who supported stable family units. The consequences had powerful long term effects on the relationships between men and women. No longer viewed as the weaker sex, men increasingly became confused between treating a woman as a lady or a competitive adversary.

When government social programs made it possible to survive without a man in the house, men became passive and drifted away from their role as fathers. The collapse of a stable family unit inevitably spilled over into the society at large as the hidden cost of the federal social programs created the demand for more social programs. Today the biggest social problem facing our nation is a lack of fathers for the children they sire as single moms juggle raising their kids while working to sustain themselves. Left to their own means, young people drifted into crime. substance abuse and poor lifestyle choices instead of building better lives for themselves. Unattached males who grew up in fatherless homes fill our prisons like no other group of people. America's biggest social problem is a lack the influence of a father at home. It's not just a problem for men but also for women who refuse to be mothers or traditional wives. No social contract of marriage can long survive when couples are locked in a power struggle.

When right becomes wrong, the people suffer in choas.

Until right becomes might and the people are free again.

We went wrong 100 years ago when our government ignored its traditionally limited role and began to intervene into the lives of its citizens. These changes actually came at the bequest of the voters believing the myth that the rich are getting rich at the expense of the poor. The real culprit is the replacement of our historical appreciation for personal liberty for easy government money. People were learning to vote for a living instead of depending on our traditional American trait of self reliance. It became nothing short of a classical sellout for a little security at the expense of personal liberty as warned by none other than James Madison, the father of our constitution.

Abraham Lincoln gave this explanation about our resolve for liberty, in a speech made at Edwardsville, Illinois, September 12, 1858;

> *What constitutes the bulwark of our own liberty and independence? It is not our frowning battlements or bristling seacoasts, or army and navy. These are not our reliance against tyranny. All of these may be turned against us without making us weaker for the struggle. Our reliance is in the love of liberty which God has planted in us. Our defense is in the spirit which prized liberty as the heritage of all men, in all lands everywhere. Destroy this spirit and you have planted the seeds of despotism at your own doors.*

The spirit of liberty had been bought with blood was now being destroyed by the temporary euphoria of easy government handouts.

How was this done? It was during FDR's extended term of office that the Keynesian economic theory was accepted the answer to faltering economies. Instead of stimulating the economy, the theory in practice created a class of political supporters who became dependent on government tax dollars to support them. This dependency served to ensure sufficient votes to re-elect the politicians expanding the bureaucracy that continues to eat away at our after-tax income with an ever-increasing appetite. After all, who would vote against someone who gave government hand-outs to them in the form of tax-paid guaranteed benefits?

This massive redistribution of wealth by our Federal government follows the same social pattern proposed by the philosophy of Karl Marx. He wrote a three volume set, <u>Das Capital</u> in which he explains his theory of how capitalism will eventually fail. He reasoned that the shortcomings of capitalism would lead to the ultimate evolution of the economy in absolute communism. Following his Communist Manifesto plan, the redistribution of the wealth from the rich to the poor was a necessary step to advance the process. Although Marx didn't keep a regular job, relying on the independent wealth of a friend, he felt qualified to condemn capitalism as evil. He refused to acknowledge the positive effects of capitalism and its ability to self correct the highs and lows of economic cycles. [36]

The adaptation of the progressive socialist formula created even more government debt. The national budget hadn't been balanced between the Eisenhower presidency in the 1950s until 1994. The one party stranglehold by the Democrats control of the House of Representatives was sustained for 40 years from 1954 to 1994. The liberal tax and spend philosophy of this legislative body has remained unchanged while the executive office had gone through several major political shifts. Unfortunately, many Americans measure our government's progress on the basis of the presidency when the unchanging Congress is actually responsible for most of our country's economic troubles.

President John F. Kennedy's economic vision was that a rising tide raises all boats. As President in 1960, he introduced tax cuts on income and investments. The ensuing years of prosperity produced the same economic expansion and government revenues as observed by Andrew Mellon 40 years earlier. Although Kennedy's presidency was tragically cut short by an assassin, his tax cuts lifted the standard of living and the spirits of all Americans that prevailed until after we landed astronauts on the moon.

Kennedy was seceded by his Vice President Lyndon Johnson who followed the plan of FDR in the Keynesian economic model. He declared war on poverty to raise the standard of living for poor Americans. The original plan would cost a total of $70 Billion. True to form government programs take on a life of their own. Now 50 years later Johnson's welfare programs have cost over $24 trillion or about the size of our current national debt. Typical to most of our national projects the increase in spending failed to make any difference in the rate of poverty. Quite to the contrary, the economic growth of the 50s and 60s did more to eradicate poverty than the government giveaways from 1970 through 2016. Tragically, the past 50 years have shown that more the government spends on social programs, the worse our society gets. There has is no exit strategy on President Johnson's War on Poverty.

Johnson other war was in Viet Nam. America's role in the conflict started under Kennedy but was ramped up by Johnson. After the assassination of Kennedy, a paranoid Johnson perceived the murder of JFK as a Communist plot. The advances of the communists into South Viet Nam need to be halted to prevent a domino effect of other South East Asian countries who were friendly to the U.S. The more he tried to micro manage the tactical plans of the war from the Oval Office, the worse it got. Running out of tax revenues, his began to borrow from the locked box of the Social Security Trust Fund to fund his war plans. When America's TV news anchorman, Walter Kronkite, told the his national tv audience on the 6 o'clock news that we were losing the war, our military began to lose the public's confidence. Gradually the public's backing for the Viet Nam war turned to open opposition.

The economic slowdowns of the 1970 were a predictable reaction to Johnson's bungling of fighting two wars at the same time. Stagnation, inflation, gasoline rationing, and high unemployment characterized the decade. Presidents Nixon was elected in 1972 and the promises of an improved economy fell flat. The Watergate scandal forced Nixon to resign. Reporters became empowered as they now saw themselves as the new power brokers in Washington. Journalists became progressive activists by favorably reporting on politicians who shared their beliefs while attacking anyone who presented as a traditional conservative. As a new generation of journalists rose to the new media, news was not as important as views. Competition for breaking news stories, often meant injecting political bias into the conventional wisdom of the daily mass media productions.

The economy of stagflation characterized the Presidents Ford and Carter's terms as as they muddled their way through their various plans that yielded little economic growth.

By 1980, private manufacturing had slowed to a trickle amid growing foreign market competition. Industrial America was breathing its last as debt and governmental safety and environmental regulations finally succeeded in strangling our businesses into a non-competitive market positions. Enter President Ronald Reagan in 1980. His pledge to cut taxes on income and investments turned into action within two years. The economy immediately began to rebound. Revenues poured into the treasury.

Yet, the widespread use of consumer credit due to Congressional deregulation of our banks created a false sense of economic security for the new "service" economy. Meanwhile the increased demand for high-tech and high priced Cold War weapons sparked yet another era of borrowed prosperity.

The surpluses could have been used to pay back the Social Security Trust fund and reduce the national debt. Instead the Democrat controlled Congress accelerated their spending plans and drove us only further into debt. Reagan's defense policies ended the tensions with the former Soviet Union when it collapsed under the inefficiencies of their communist economic model. Consumer caution became lost in this decade of greed. With discipline and thrift thrown to the wind, personal and government debt soared just like it did in the 1920s. Reaganomics sustained a robust economy well into the early 1990s when President George H Bush allowed the Democrats to once again raised taxes on successful Americans. His broken pledge of "read my lips, no new taxes" sank his re-election bid in 1992 to Bill Clinton another tax and spend democrat. By 1994, American voters had enough of the liberal spending policies and ended the 40 year rule of the Democrats. In the House of Representatives. Republican victories in Congress translated into tax cuts fueling another boom in the economy. Government revenues increased and a balanced budget was finally achieved. Buoyed by their successes the moderate Republicans abandoned their principles and proceeded to raising taxes and spending federal money just like the Democrats before them. The economy began to slow down yet again.

By 2000, the voters again had enough of the high taxes, and

elected George W. Bush. The Bush tax cuts produced the same economic effects as those of Harding and Coolidge in the 1920s, JFK in 1960, and Ronald Reagan in 1980. Do you see the similarities? Tax cuts on income and investments are the only way to stimulate the economy and create jobs. The Bush tax cuts worked until 2008, when the government's efforts to provide affordable house to people who couldn't repay their mortgages created a tsunami of financial losses in the financial markets around the world. Once again feel good government programs caused massive economic chaos in the economy.

After 80 years of government hand outs, corporate bailouts, regulatory interventions, business and personal debt, our economy had become entrapped in another economic quagmire. Gas prices soared to $4 per gallon in July of 2008 thanks to environ-friendly Democrats who blocked the expansion of new oil wells in America.

Increased U.S. dependency on foreign oil left us vulnerable to the policies of unfriendly oil cartels. Meanwhile, the Chinese consumption of oil dramatically increased the demand and the price of crude skyrocketed. The American economy headed south while Democrats blocked new energy resources. The stock market tanked taking with it half of the nation's retirement investments. By 2009 the economy went into a tail spin bottoming out in the worst depression since the Great Depression if the 1930s.

The election of President Obama in 2008 promised "Change we can believe in". By playing on the rich get richer lie, the Democrats won back control of both houses of Congress with a commanding majority. However Obama's change was not what we expected. In spite of Obama's radical spending plans to bail out politically friendly businesses and threats of a tax hike on Americans making over $250,000 per year, the combined effect blocked a struggling economy from rebounding. The Obama solution was to continue to borrow money to spend on more social programs to redistribute America's wealth while expanding the regulatory bureaucracy. All of this uncontrolled government spending increased the national debt to $18 trillion dollars up from 4 trillion in only ten years. A debt that must be repaid with real dollars if we are to avoid an economic earthquake. God help the next generations who will be saddled with this problem.

Remember the golden rule? **He who holds the gold; rules.** Our country has been selling treasury notes to the Communist Chinese government who expect to be repaid with interest. Imagine what would happen if the Chinese decided to call in all of the notes? They could crash our economy. Remember how the Soviet Union fell without firing a shot? It was their unsustainable debt that caused their economy to fail before the government collapsed. Who is responsible for this unprecedented debacle? The liberal progressives attitudes possessed by career politicians who buy elections with earmarks from Washington, D.C. while the media protects them from scrutiny and attacks the conservatives who disagree with the progressive agenda.

Interestingly the Russians and most of the former iron curtain satellite countries of the former Soviet Union dropped communism and adapted capitalist economic policies beginning with low flat income tax rates. The economies of these countries immediately experienced a rebound. Capitalism worked even where communism failed.

Enter the election of Donald Trump as a president 2016. He set about cutting taxes and regulations as never before in this country. The results were predictable, The economy took off. The stock market nearly doubled in only three years. Wages in all sectors rose. New jobs were created and welfare rolls dropped. However the long term damages to the social structure would not recover as quickly as they eventually will if the people look within and heal themselves and their families.

When right is might, the people are free

CHAPTER 11. AMERICAN LIBERTY TODAY.

Man's inhumanity to his fellow man is a sign of personal moral disorder. Widespread indifference or injury to others is a sign of social disorder. A statistical measure of criminal behavior is measured by the incidence of criminal acts committed by the population, the crime rate. An increasing crime rate means the personal or collective conscience has a diminishing control over human behavior towards others. Violent crime is a particularly onerous mark of social and moral confusion. Anarchy is total political confusion, the exact opposite of civil order. And finally, war is wanton political violence.

To the contrary, crime doesn't occur when there is love and respect among people. Morally rooted people do not normally engage in criminal acts. Therefore the key to social order is in the cultivation and preservation of a morally based personal conscience.

The validity of any political theory lies in its ability to withstand the test of time. Consider the consequences of the rapid increases in politically correct social spending driven by the liberal progressive socialists. We now have;

12 year olds given condoms by our teachers.
13 year olds carrying guns to school.
14 year olds having abortions.
15 year olds addicted to drugs.

16 year olds killing one another.

17 year olds dying of AIDS.

18 year olds who are functionally illiterate.

19 year olds who can't keep a job.

20 year olds filing for divorce.

21 year olds committing suicide.

30 to 50 year olds dying of drug and alcohol overdoses.

65 year olds filing for bankruptcy.

70 and 80 year olds abandoned and seeking euthanasia or suicide,

Why is this happening in our country? We have all seen the media headlines describe the gloomy news of violent domestic crime, racial riots, hatred towards our police, suppression of conservative voices, attacks against the people of faith, uncontrolled public spending, and a 21 trillion dollar national debt. The states and the cities are just as bad. Simultaneous with the economic woes are the reports of increases in drug and alcohol abuse, declining marriage rates and the lowest birth rate in modern times, high divorce rates and the now the China covid 19 virus pandemic.

If a tree falls in the woods and no one hears it fall, did it really make any noise? The same can be said about our national media. If no one hears or sees the fake news media is it really news under the freedom of the press?

One wonders how much of the only industry specifically protected by the first amendment contributes to the decline in civility in our communities. With the advent of the 24/7/365 cable news organizations, the explosive growth of social media "news" and the internet, the freedom of the press has become a source of dark news intended to misinform truth and promote false information to steer the public with their leftist narratives. It's not the first time these tactics have been employed by media moguls intent on steering the good ship America to their liking.

Mark Twain once wrote that a lie could go around the world two times before truth ties its shoe laces. Propaganda does just that. But as President Lincoln was credited to say that "You can fool all of the people some of the time. Some of the people all the time, but you can't fool all of the people all of the time."

Tragically our traditional moral heritage, which has historically kept a internal check on our collective behavior, is being systematically removed by a tiny minority under the false constitutional authority to propagandize under the guise of a free press. Without the collective influence of the church on public affairs, the trend will continue as progressives demand that the people of faith be silenced by the absolute separation of church and state.

When these economic, social, and religious issues are in conflict the end result is always violent. The connection between them is simple; dysfunctional group behavior. Most social scientists will agree that the principle reason for most of today's social ills are directly related to broken human relationships mostly from within the families. Violent and property crime, drug and alcohol abuse, teenage pregnancies, runaways, the homeless, and even more divorce can be traced to being raised among dysfunctional or fractured families.

Other social studies clearly show that finances are the principle cause of trouble within marriages. Traditional two parent families are better able to manage themselves then single parent families simply because two parents have more resources than one. So why then would the liberal progressives encourage single parenthood with welfare handouts? Why would our government reward something that contributes to perpetual social problems?

Our progressive career politicians have been able to subjugate this vulnerable portion of the population by creating a dependence on government sponsored programs. The poverty pimps circle these programs like vultures feeding off of the ignorance of the masses. Earning money by working was the traditional way people learn the value of it. Welfare money circumvents that learning experience because recipients haven't earned it. Government workers encourage more unwitting dependents to join in the welfare trap in order to preserve their union jobs.

Unfortunately the net effect of government dependance is similar to drug dependance. The taste of free dollars allures the recipient to ask for more of the same tax-supported hand outs. The price of financial dependency can not be satisfied without an abrupt reversal of behavior. However change means pain. The government addict gets the money needed to barely survive and the pusher/politicians get re-elected. The clever cycle of co-dependance creates a permanent Congress and a monopoly over the power of Washington!

What has yet to be seen is the problem of our enormous private debts. The cost of indulgence is far reaching. Our interest payments to the banks consume what would normally have been saved or donated to charities. Americans have been known for their generosity. Yet, as the social conscious has been stolen by the progressive politicians from the traditional caretakers of the poor, i.e. the people of faith, the perceived responsibility for the less-advantaged has been transferred to government. And of course the government pays for these services with higher tax rates which reduces the amount of charitable contributions from benevolent citizens. Another progressive trick on to expand the power of government at the expense of our liberties.

Presently, it is estimated that more than 60% of our citizens receive more government benefits than they pay for in taxes. How is that fair to those who get less than what they pay in taxes? What is fair anyhow? Why is government fairness, aka social justice, so important to be forcibly extracted from the most generous people in history?

The preamble of the Constitution calls for "providing for the common defense and promoting the general welfare" Liberal progressive politicians have inverted the constitutional directive to "promote the common defense and provide for the general welfare." America's self reliance has become government reliance costing $21 trillion since the Great Society programs of the 1960s. The national debt for social programs is nearly three times the combined costs of all of America's wars since the founding. Instead of protecting Americans from our enemies and encouraging people to depend on themselves and God's ability to provide, our elected officials want our citizens to depend upon them while they play God.

But when the Government can no longer deliver on its promises, people are left without money and hope. Just as drug addicts avoid cold turkey withdrawals by desperately searching for the next fix, government dependents will become desperate and possibly violent. A soaring crime rate and big government are related because social disorientation is the root cause of crime.

How did this all begin?

The key here is Franklin Roosevelt's unprecedented four terms of office. By ignoring the example of past presidents going back to George Washington, FDR began a pattern for career politicians of the future to follow. The damage to our liberties which came from this prolonged control of a public office lead to the 22nd Amendment in 1951. This constitutional amendment forever limited the president to two only terms of office. Its too bad that they didn't limit the terms of office for the Congress.

Later, the Senate and the House of Representatives would abuse their privileges by remaining in office far too long. For this reason the same liberal, progressives in the Democrat party has maintained control of the House of Representatives for decades. That's not a republic of limited government or even a stable democracy, it is a House of Lords!

There is plenty of this kind of historical proof to warn us that the most dangerous threat to our personal liberty and individual freedom is the unbridled encroachment of government into our lives. Over the past half century, the gradual, finely-engineered expansion of government control over our lives has created in its path nearly 100 federal agencies. The most immediate problem facing all Americans is the mind-boggling cost of sustaining this beast. For the past several years, the U.S. Congress spent trillions more than what was budgeted. When this debt is added to the previous unpaid balance to feed our federal monster, the total amounts to over $21 trillion tax dollars or $21,000,000,000,000.00. The interest payments for this debt approaches 50% of all of the income taxes collected.

To give the reader some idea of the enormity of this debt, consider what would have happened if Adam and Eve were to begin to spend 2 million dollars per day above their needs 6000 years ago. If their descendants could continue to spend that same amount for each of the 365 days of the past 6000 years, then they would have spent the equivalent that which our permanent Congress has spent in only the past two years!

Alarmingly, the operations of this vast empire of bureaucracy have virtually replaced the legislative activity of the Congress! Currently, our elected representatives are hard-pressed to find time for anything more than insuring preservation of the status quo. Status quo here really means, more government programs and more government agencies spending more and more of our tax dollars.

Why has this happened? The socialist policies of the permanent Congress has eroded our individual liberty and has diluted our work ethic with discouraging regulations and the systematic removal of Christian morals from our government.

Clearly, the most dangerous threat to personal liberty and individual freedom in America looms in the vast complex of government agencies writing policies to insulate power from change. There is a deadly thread attached to every policy that provides a government handout. Government control always follows government tax dollars handed out under the false notion of acting in the public interest. Whenever the government does something FOR us, more government CONTROL comes to bear on our individual freedoms and we end up with fewer liberties than we had previously.

How do we solve these political mess? By re-establishing morality in government by recruiting and supporting candidates who will restore our traditional principles of limiting the size of the federal government. And to return to the checks and balances as established in our constitution which ensures a competitive political process, not a permanent legislative body. It is now become obvious that the only solution to the permanent congress is to amend the constitution to limit the terms of all elected officials just as the presidency had to be limited. We have no other choice, the Congress will not limit itself. The task, therefore, falls on the shoulders of the voters in the states to force the state legislators to introduce a constitutional amendment as provided in Article 5 as had been done with the Bill of Rights in 1789. When 2/3 or 34 states pass proposals to change the constitution, they will get an opportunity to permanently ratify it.

Sadly, we are no longer a republic, nor are we even a democracy.

Only a minority of all Americans bother to vote. When the control of our government is determined by a minority, it becomes obvious that the majority no longer rules.

Until right becomes might and the people are free again.

CHAPTER 12. LIBERTY IN AMERICA'S FUTURE

The final episode of personal freedom and liberty in America could very well be written by you. It is my sincere hope that the reader will not quickly dismiss those ominous warnings that are already present on the American political scene. I would hope that Americans would act now while there is still time to arrest the beast that will threaten our personal liberties. The one weapon we all must use to bring this runaway government to a halt is for the individual to cast an educated vote in all of our national and local elections. Recall that it was a dedicated minority that defeated the British during the American War for Independence.

As was noted by the writer of the ancient book of Ecclesiastes, there is truly "...nothing new under the sun." The phrase is very appropriate for politics. What is often thought to be new in politics is, in reality old, even ancient.

Consider the range of ideas advanced by Plato, Aristotle, Hobbes, Rousseau, Locke, Jefferson, and Madison. The same questions have been addressed by each; who should run our societies? Should the role be exclusively fulfilled by government itself or by individuals to whom the government is accountable?

From a strictly historical perspective, the collapsed empires of ancient Egypt, Babylon, Greece, and Rome have provided a sufficient amount of evidence as to why governments and their societies fail.

These past governments failed because of public and private debt, inflation, moral disintegration, collapse of the home, divorces leading to the dissolution of the family unit, a failure of education, political indifference, corruption, lying, extortion, embezzlement, and a rejection of a common god. Although history reveals the United States to be the longest lasting Republic, but we are not immune to the same kinds of social disintegrations that destroyed these other empires.

Let us once again listen to some qualified voices from the past.

The renowned 19th Century French philosopher Alexis De Toqueville, who traveled extensively throughout our country, may have made the most accurate commentary about America's greatness;

> *I searched for the greatness and genius of America in her commodious harbors and anchored whalers. And it was not there. In her fertile fields and boundless prairies and it was not there. In her rich minds and her vast world of commerce and it was not there. Not until I went to the churches of America and heard her pulpits aflame with righteousness, did I understand the secret of her success. America is great because she is good and if America ever ceases to be good, America will cease to be great.*

We should all wonder what happened to the America that President John F. Kennedy addressed in his Inaugural, when he urged; *"Ask not what your country can do for you. Ask what you can do for your country."*

Today we are confronted with a Congress bent upon expanding the federal beast at an ever-increasing rate, a huge federal bureaucracy buoyed up by excessive taxation, with the result that we have become to believe that only our Federal government can solve all our problems. At the same time our activist media pundits have repeatedly attempted to frustrated any morally based reforms in government. It is downright impossible for the current government we have in place in Washington to find a way out of the mess created by its own hands, when the only feasible political solution in sight means spending ourselves into bankruptcy and possibly oblivion.

How long will we continue to ignore the fact that as individuals, we are expected to live within a budget, yet we support a government that refuses to balance its own finances? Perhaps it is the deliberate conspiracy by the liberal progressive socialists who are attempting to carry out the plans of Karl Marx to institute a progressive, graduated income tax until all people have the same amount of money. Yet the experiences of the former Soviet Union clearly demonstrate the failure of communism. Oddly, most western countries who have experimented with socialism are abandoning it while our country is heading down the same failed path.

It is truly ironic that we're asking the same beast that presented America with an equally enormous debt to solve the problem of liberal socialist spending. It's something like asking the fox to watch over the hen house.

Our history of an ever expanding Federal Government demonstrates that it does not get out of debt by levying more and more tax dollars for more and more political solutions that don't work. During the past 100 years, only solutions that have increased the government's revenues have been to lower taxes at all levels which spurs economic growth adding employment for more taxpayers. That solution, used by William Harding, Calvin Cooledge, John Kennedy, Ronald Reagan, the 1994 Republican Congress and George W. Bush, and now Donald Trump is to reduce taxes on income and investments. However tax cuts must accompany a reduction in government spending.

Under the Obama administration, progressive politicians in Congress have only found more ways to spend, this time it is money borrowed from our former enemies or to simply create more digital dollars.

The consequences of printing more money has been tried before with devastating effects. This political solution to debt has been used in Germany after the first World War, more recently in Argentina and in the former Soviet Union. The disastrous results were rather predictable; the economies of each of those nations collapsed. First by creeping inflation then hyper-inflation. Germany's solution was Adolf Hitler.

How does more money cause such an inflationary increase in prices?

When the government prints more money it means that the money that one already has must compete with the increased competition to buy a fixed amount of goods and services. The competition created by the extra available money forces people with real money to spend more for less because the increased demand for a product whose scarcity increases its price. This happens when there are more buyers than products, the higher bidders will get the goods. When this scenario happens throughout the economy it is called inflation. If this inflation gets out of hand it become hyperinflation.

Hyperinflation means that the prices for goods and services is increasing at an annual rate of 100% or higher. The rapid changes in prices causes a panic that drives people to spend their money faster and faster in order to stretch their ability to buy at the current prices before they increase again. The hoarding causes a rapid acceleration of spending until desperation forces people to use their savings to stay even. This continues until the savings are exhausted. The extraordinary demand of certain items further drives the price spiral because of the increased market demand for a diminishing supply of products. The net effect of hyperinflation is that it will destroy the savings and pension plans of the middle class.

Remember that these dollars were saved on the assumption that tomorrow's dollar will be worth about as much as the dollar that was saved. If tomorrow's dollar is worth less than the saved dollar, the investor loses the full worth of his efforts to collect and invest the money.

How do we solve this national problem?

Have we forgotten the good men and women who have made this country what she is today? Have we forgotten the foundational values of our constitutional republic?

Remember what was said about our Biblically based capitalist roots? Well, capitalism will work again if people handle their property including their money, in a responsible and predictable fashion. If the average person will not act responsibly with their capital, the government will act. Such a situation is called a command economy where property, wages and supplies are centrally controlled by the government. One only has to be reminded of the collapse of Eastern Europe's economy to realize that the command method is a failure.

The same tragedy could happen in America if we don't put a stop to the insane dependency on government and its wild spending habits. We should not place our trust in the temporary promises of the permanent Congressional politicians to provide "womb to tomb" solutions for the majority of the voters. Our trust must be in the God of our Founding Fathers, the same great provider, the Jehovah of the Judeo-Christian tradition.

In light of our problems, consider these quotations;

> *The budget should be balanced, the treasury should be refilled, and the public debt should be reduced. The arrogance of officialdom should be tempered and controlled. And the assistance to foreign lands should be curtailed, lest we become bankrupt.*

Cicero in 63 B.C.

> *A democracy is not a form of government to survive. For it will only succeed until its citizens discover they can vote themselves money from the treasury, then they will bankrupt it.*

Karl Marx.

By direct contrast, consider what President Grover Cleveland had to say about the practice of government hand-outs.

> *It is the responsibility of the citizens to support their government. It is not the responsibility of the government to support its citizens.*

Cleveland's views were those of traditional America. Unfortunately, government wants to support its citizens with borrowed money. The power of government in the modern era has become the power of money. This control over money also has become a form of control over our personal liberties. Consider the following quotation from Amermica's first progressive president, Woodrow Wilson.

The history of liberty is a history of limitations of governmental power, not the increase of it. When we resist, therefore, the concentration of power, we are resisting the powers of death, because concentration of power is what always precedes the destruction of human liberties.

Now the same quotation using today's language.

The history of liberty is a history of limiting the power of governments to spend the citizen's taxes, not the increase of taxes. When we resist, therefore, the concentration of money, we are resisting the powers of poverty, because the concentration of money is what always precedes the destruction of human economic liberties.

Thomas Jefferson was acutely aware of the need to limit the powers of our government, so he cautioned all generations of Americans;

In questions of power then let no more be heard of confidence of man, but bind him down from mischief by the chains of the Constitution.

Jefferson was also aware that if governments were not enslaved, the people ruled by them eventually would be. This morally painful result of unbridled government was no doubt one of the consequences that Jefferson envisioned when he expressed the view that *"government governs best that governs least."*

If the powers that threaten our United States Constitution on every front are ultimately successful, the nearly complete erosion of our individual freedom will be assured. When the very document providing freedom is altered or diluted in its principle form, we can only expect that individual liberty will suffer. It was a constitutional republic of limited government our Founding Fathers envisioned when they drew up our Constitution, whereas today we are continuing to gravitate toward a total government.

Yet, one may ask, "but which party can solve the problem?"

Neither party has all of the answers. However, the presence of opposing views is necessary for keeping the political arena fresh with new politicians with constitutional ideals. Whenever one party completely dominates the political environment for an extended period of time, stagnation invariably sets in. The results of such a political monopoly is laziness, dullness and incompetence. Such a monopoly tends to breed "fat cats" and political dynasties that have characterized tyrannical governments of the past, simply because all of their competition has been silenced.

James Madison's commentary in Federalist 37 may have stated the case most clearly about the need for limiting terms of office.

The genius of Republican liberty, seems to demand on one side, not only that all power should be derived from the people; but that those entrusted with it should be kept in dependence on the people, by a short duration of their appointments; and, that, even during this short period, the trust should be placed not in a few, but in a number of hands...

And again in Federalist 53.

It is a received and well founded maxim, that, where no other circumstances affect the case, the greater the power is, the shorter ought to be its duration.

We must all take a stand to prevent the progressive actors in our permanent Congress from further robbing Americans of their liberty and their money. And we must act quickly.

The available solutions are these;

#1. Vote AGAINST incumbent politicians.

#2. Vote FOR state legislative candidates who will propose a constitutional amendment to limit the terms of office for the Federal Congress.

#3. Vote FOR state legislative candidates who will propose a constitutional amendment to require a balanced federal budget with a line item veto for the president.

#4. Vote FOR state legislative candidates who will propose a constitutional amendment to require a flat federal income tax will contain the federal spending instead of the current progressive socialist graduated method for income taxes.

#5. Vote FOR candidates who honor our traditional American values found in our unique constitution and our Christian heritage.

And while the memory of this great abuse of our government is still fresh in the minds of the voters, we must insist on a binding law to prevent another similar debacle. The only solution is a constitutional amendment by 2/3 or 34 of the state legislatures.

The twenty-eighth Amendment to the U.S. Constitution could read as such:

AMENDMENT XXVIII.

> Section 1. No person shall be elected more than three terms to the House of Representatives, including special elections. Senators shall be appointed by the various state legislatures by a majority vote.

> Section 2. Income taxes rates shall be fair to all by requiring a flat rate for all the citizens. The annual budget must be balanced on the revenues except in times of war. Any changes in this rate must be approved by the Congress. The President may veto any portion of a proposed budget as deemed necessary.

> Section 3. This amendment shall be inoperative unless it has been ratified as an amendment to the Constitution by the legislatures of three-fourths of the several states within seven years after it has been approved by the Congress.

It is my sincere hope that the treasured prize of liberty for Americans will continue through the next century. I pray that the proposed constitutional amendment will be able to secure our future from the tyranny of government money and preserve our "liberty and justice for all."

> *When might is right, the people groan in bondage.*

> *When right is might, the people are free.*

> *When right becomes wrong, the people suffer in chaos.*

> *Until right becomes might and the people are free again.*

Willeam A Choby DMD MPA   June 2020

"The happy Union of these States is a wonder:
their Constitution a miracle:
their example the hope of Liberty throughout the world"

James Madison. Father of the U.S. Constitution

ENDNOTES:

1   https://patternsofevidence.com
2   http://classics.mit.edu/Plato/republic.html
3   http://classics.mit.edu/Aristotle/politics.html
4   http://www.camelotintl.com/village/society.html
5   http://www.historylink101.com/middle_ages_europe/middle_ages_daily_life.htm
6   http://www.eh-resources.org/timeline/timeline_lia.html
7   http://www.themiddleages.net/plague.html
8   http://www.constitution.org/sr/lexrex.htm
9   http://www.constitution.org/jjr/socon_04.htm#009
10 https://fee.org/articles/john-locke-natural-rights-to-life-liberty-and-property
11 https://www.britannica.com/topic/The-Social-Contract
12 http://westfordknight.blogspot.com
13 http://whatscookingamerica.net/History/PotatoHistory.htm
14 https://en.wikipedia.org/wiki/Squanto
15 http://www.ratical.com/many_worlds/6Nations/index.html
16 https://www.findagrave.com/memorial/28267426
17 https://founders.archives.gov/?q=Author%3A%22Washington%2C%20George%22%20Period%3A%22Colonial%22&s=1111311113&r=56
18 Http://www.mapsofpa.com/18thcentury/s522.jpg with permission from mapsofpa.com.
19 https://www.smithsonianmag.com/history/when-young-george-washington-started-war-180973076/
20 http://www.reversespins.com/bulletproof.html
21 http://www.allabouthistory.org/mayflower-compact.htm
22 http://www.sparknotes.com/history/american/prerevolution/section1.html
23 http://www.earlyamerica.com/review/winter96/enlargement.html "Courtesy of the Early American Digital Library"
24 http://www.eyewitnesstohistory.com/teaparty.htm

25   http://www.nationalcenter.org/PaulRevere%27sRide.html
26   http://www.eyewitnesstohistory.com/lexington.htm
27   http://www.earlyamerica.com/earlyamerica/milestones/commonsense
28   http://www.ushistory.org/declaration/document/index.htm
29   http://libertyonline.hypermall.com/ArtConfed.htm.
30   http://www.answers.com/topic/american-revolutionary-war
31   http://www.myrevolutionarywar.com
32   http://www.foundingfathers.info/federalistpapers/
33   http://www.archives.gov/historical-docs/document.html?doc=3&title.raw=
     Constitution of the United States
34   https://billofrightsinstitute.org/founding-documents/bill-of-rights/
35   http://www.livinghistoryfarm.org/farminginthe30s/water_02.html
36   http://plato.stanford.edu/entries/marx

BIBLIOGRAPHIC ROOTS:

I began to prepare this book long before I ever decided to write it. I would rather describe the process as an attempt to satisfy my personal curiosity. It was during this process that I had the opportunity to read, watch, or listen to literally hundreds of contemporary and historical references, both in pursuit of my Masters degree in Public Administration and in preparation for my political campaigns. The following materials served as the foundation of my beliefs and opinions.

Marshall, Peter and David Manuel, The Light and the Glory, (Fleming H. Revell Co., Tarrytown, New York, 1977).

Marshall, Peter and David Manuel, From Sea To Shining Sea, (Fleming H. Revell Co. Tarrytown, New York, 1986).

Kennedy, Paul, The Rise and Fall of Great Powers, (New York, Random House, 1987).

Burkett, Larry, The Coming Economic Earthquake, (Moody Press, Chicago, Ill., 1990.)

The Rebuilding of America (Authur DeMoss Foundation, St. David's Pa., 1986).

Colson, Chuck and Jack Eckerd, <u>Why America Doesn't Work</u>, (Word Publishing, Dallas, 1991).

Nisbet, Robert, <u>The Social Philosophers,</u> (Washington Square Press, New York, 1973).

Noorbergen, Rene and Ralph W. hood, <u>The Death Cry of an Eagle</u>, (Grand Rapids, Mi., Zondervan Publishing House, 1980).

LaHaye, Tim, <u>Faith of Our Founding Fathers</u>, Brentwood, Tn, Wolgemuth & Hyatt Publishers, 1987)

McGuire, Paul, <u>Who Will Rule the Future</u>, (Lafayette, La., Huntington House Publishers, 1991).

Whitemarsh, Darylann, <u>We Can Change America</u>, Hannibal, Mo, Hannibal Books, 3rd Ed., 1992).

Smith, William Jennings, <u>God in Our Government</u>, (Little Rock, Ak, Pioneer Press, 1985).

Smith, Adam, <u>The Wealth of Nations, Books I-III</u>, Edited by Andrew Skinner, (London, Penquin Books, Reprinted 1776 edition in 1986).

Rohr, John, <u>To Run A Constitution</u>, (Lawrence, Ks, University of Kansas Press, 1986)

Kelly, Alfred, Winfred A. Harbison and Herman Belz, <u>The American Constitution</u>, 6th Edition, (New York, W.W. Norton & Co., 1983)

Barna, George, <u>What Americans Believe</u>, (Ventura, Ca, Regal Books, 1991)

<u>The Moral Foundations of the American Republic</u>, 3rd ed., Edited by Robert H. Horwitz, (Charlottesville, Va., University Press of Virginia, 1986)

Woll, Peter, <u>American Bureaucracy</u>, 2nd Ed. (New York, W.W. Norton & Co., 1977)

Hamilton, Alexander, James Madison and John Jay, The Federalist, Edited by Jacob E. Cooke, (Middletown, Ct., Wesleyan University Press, 1961)

Holy Bible From the Ancient Eastern Text, translated by George Lamsa from the Aramaic of the Peshitta, (San Francisco, Ca., Harper & Row, 1933)

Hardy, Dorcas, and C. Colburn Hardy, Social Insecurity, (New York, Villard Books, 1991).

Amos, Gary, Defending the Declaration, (Brentwood, Tn., Wolgemuth and Hyatt, 1989)

Jones, Charles O., An Introduction to the Study of Public Policy, 3rd Ed. (Monterey, Ca., Brooks/Cole Publishing Co., 1984).

Skowronek, Stephen, Building a New American State, (Cambridge University Press, 1984)

Bureaucrats, Policy Analysts, Statesmen, Who Leads?, Edited by Robert A. Goldwin, (Washington, D.C., American Enterprise Institute, 1980).

Mosher, Frederick C., Democracy and the Public Service, 2nd ed. (New York, Oxford Press, 1982).

Walter, Susan and Pat Choate, Thinking Strategically, A primer for Public Leaders, (Washington, D.C., The Council of State Planning Agencies, 1984).

French, Wendell, and Cecil H. Bell, Jr., Organizational Development, 3rd ed. (Englewood Cliffs, NJ., Prentice-Hall, Inc., 1984).

Shafritz, Jay M., Albert C. Hyde, and David H. Rosenbloom, Personnel Management in Government, 3rd ed., (New York, Marcel Dekker, Inc., 1986).

Stewart, Debra W., G. David Garson, Organizational Behavior and Public Management, (New York, Marcel Dekker, Inc., 1983).

Varian, Hal R., Intermediate Microeconomics, (New York, W.W. Norton & Co., 1987).

Dunn, William N., Public Policy Analysis, An Introduction, (Englewood Cliffs, NJ., Prentice-Hall, Inc., 1981).

Meltsner, Arnold J., Policy Analysts in the Bureaucracy, (Berkley, Ca., University of California Press, 1976).

McKenna, Christopher K., Quantitative Methods for Public Decision Making, (New York, McGraw-Hill Book Co., 1980).

Bennis, Warren G., Kenneth D. Benne, and Robert Chin, The Planning of Change, 4th ed., (New York, Holt, Rhinehart and Winston, 1985).

Macdonald, Charles R., MBO can Work! How to Manage by Contract, (New York, McGraw-Hill Book Co., 1982).

White, Michael J., et al., Managing Public Systems, (Lanham, MD., University Press of America, 1985).

Kingdon, John W., Agendas, Alternatives, and Public Policies, (Boston, MA., Little, Brown and Company, 1984).

Rohr, John A., Ethics for Bureaucrats, (New York, Marcel Dekker, Inc., 1978).

Kelley, Joseph T., Costing Government Services: A Guide for Decision Making, (Washington, D.C., Government Finance Research Center, 1984).

Shafritz, Jay M., Albert C. Hyde, Classics of Public Administration, (Oak Park, IL., Moore Publishing Co., 1978).

Ethics and Politics, Edited by Amy Gutmann and Dennis Thompson, (Chicago, Il., Nelson-Hall Publishers, 1984).

Sommers, Albert T., The U. S. Economy Demystified, (Lexington, MA., D.C. Heath and Company, 1986).

Babbie, Earl, The Practice of Social Research, 4th ed., (Belmont, CA., Wadsworth Publishing Co., 1986).

Budget Management, A Reader in Local Government Financial Management, Edited by Jack Rabin, Published by Carl Vinson Institute of Government, University of Georgia, 1983.

Hardy, David T., Origins and Development of the Second Amendment, (Chino Valley, AZ., Blacksmith Inc., 1986).

Halbrook, Stephen P., That Every Man Be Armed, (Oakland CA., The Independent Institute, 1984).

Bennett, William J., The Index of Leading Cultural Indicators, Published jointly by Empower America, The Heritage Foundation, Free Congress Foundation, Washington, D. C., March 1993.

Also the following Audio or Video presentations;

"America, Your too Young to Die!, produced by the Arthur DeMoss Foundation, St. Davids, Pa. 19087, 1986.

"Taking Liberties: The Betrayal of Our Heritage", Program #9234, The Coral Ridge Ministries, Florida. 08-23-92.

"In God They Trusted", Peter Marshall and David Manuel, Crossroads Videoservices, Toronto, Ontario.

"The Story of America's Liberty", Reel to Real Ministries, Pittsburgh, Pa.

"The Giants of Political Thought", an audio cassette series by Knowledge Products, P.O. Box 305151, Nashville, Tn 37230., 1-800-876-4332.

"America's Godly Heritage" and other excellent audio/visual tapes prepared by David Barton of Wallbuilders, P.O. Box 397, Aledo, Texas 76008. 817-441-6044.